The Hanukkah Book

Mae Shafter Rockland

SCHOCKEN BOOKS
NEW YORK

This book is for Shoshanna Goodman and Benjamin Joseph Goodman

First published by Schocken Books 1975
10 9 8 7 6 5 4 3 2   85 86 87 88
Copyright © 1975, 1985 by Schocken Books Inc.

Library of Congress Cataloging in Publication Data
Rockland, Mae Shafter.
  The Hanukkah book.
  Includes index.
  1. Hanukkah decorations.   I. Title.
TT900.H34R6   745.59′41   75-10609

Photographs, except those in "Portfolio," by Jim McDonald

Manufactured in the United States of America
ISBN 0−8052−0792−9

Contents

Preface

Every November for the past few years I have received letters and calls from Jewish centers, women's groups, public schools, and libraries, requesting me to "do a program on decorations for Hanukkah" sometime in early December so that Jewish children will not feel bereft of all that sparkle and glitter associated with midwinter in the United States. This sentiment is illustrated by some lines from a lamentable children's book found in the Religion section of my daughter's public school library: "They don't make colored light bulbs/For Chanukah night./Mama said, 'Better off.'/Papa said, 'Lucky boy.'/But I knew in my heart/I was missing some joy."*

Perhaps unintentionally this little book, a product of the pressures of assimilation, reflects the tremendous alienation Jews in America feel at Christmas time. I would reply that Hanukkah is a minor festival and that decorations are not traditional for Hanukkah but rather for Sukkot and Shavuot. Both are harvest festivals: Sukkot (Festival of Tabernacles), which comes in the fall, is the holiday the Pilgrims modeled Thanksgiving after; and Shavuot (Pentecost), in the spring, comes forty days after Passover and commemorates the giving of the Law on Mount Sinai as well as the offering of the first fruits.

I must admit that my reluctance to undertake a program on Hanukkah decorations was not solely due to the lack of traditional precedents but was also colored by my intense prejudice against the usual Sunday-school type of arts and crafts program. I myself was once a Sunday school art teacher and know intimately the problems that one

*From *A Chanukah Fable for Christmas*, by Jerome Coopersmith (New York, G.P. Putnam's Sons, 1969).

faces in going from classroom to classroom, with fifteen or twenty minutes in each to "make something Jewish" as an illustration of the lesson of the week. But the fact that I was not willing to confront the situation does not mean that the desire and need for quality Hanukkah artifacts and decorations in the United States does not pose a very real and interesting set of challenges and problems. The very fact that Hanukkah craft workshops are in ever-increasing demand is an indication of the changing status of this holiday in American Jewish life.

In Israel as well as in the United States Hanukkah has changed in recent years from a minor holiday characterized by simple domestic and synagogue celebrations to a major means of expressing Jewish identity. Many Jews are appalled by the changes in Hanukkah observation, seeing in them only sellouts to commercialism and competition with Christmas. We no longer have the choice of approving or disapproving of what has happened to Hanukkah in the United States. And I can no longer comfortably retreat behind the plea that Hanukkah decorations are "not traditional." Things cannot be traditional as they are first developing and happening. Only after the event do they become invested with that special aura we associate with tradition. Changes in the celebration of Hanukkah have already occurred. The option now open to us is to make certain that the new and greater significance of Hanukkah is understood in Jewish terms rather than to let our holiday become just another part of the midwinter Christmas carnival celebrations. Thus this book is in part an attempt to counter the pernicious effects of Christmas celebration on the American Jewish mentality. I'm not ashamed of that—I don't want to make a Jewish Christmas. I want to encourage and help Jews to look more deeply into Judaic source material in order to enrich Hanukkah in an authentically Jewish way.

Every day my attention is drawn to one article after another in either the Jewish or the American press dealing with the question of Jewish identity, assimilation, and education. The tone of these articles varies from total pessimism, in which the American Jew is seen as an endangered species and the imminent disappearance of the American Jewish community is predicted, to awestruck optimism, in which the return of Jewish youth to traditional forms of Judaism such as Hasidism is recounted and seen as evidence of a Jewish Renaissance. Articles regularly appear chronicling, evaluating, interpreting, and reinterpreting conflicting sets of statistics on intermarriage and correlating or choosing to ignore the possibilities of a relationship between these statistics and the present state of Jewish education. Often these articles—although calling for more money to be spent, more studies to be made, and more support from the big Jewish charities—ultimately say that little can be done to strengthen Jewish education since there is almost no reinforcement of Jewish values in the typical Jewish-American home. We begin reading these chest-beating articles with a sense of mission and purpose, feeling that we are encountering and dealing with the dilemma of perpetuating and transmitting our Jewishness to future generations. We end by feeling guilty. Without underestimating the magnitude and weight of the problem of the survival of Jewish culture and values, I prefer not to harbor an unnecessary burden of guilt about not being observant or Jewish "enough." This is a bottomless pit that leads nowhere. I would rather redirect my energies toward taking those things that I already do and enjoy and enriching them with gleanings from my Jewish heritage. In this way I feel that I will not have an artificial separation, either in my home or in myself, between that which is Jewish and the rest of my life. We must not let the tensions between the attractions and demands of the secular world and those of our Jewish lives distract us from putting our creative energy into making a contribution to a vibrant Jewish-American culture.

The reader, leafing through this book, may well be puzzled to find on one page a stuffed denim dreidel, on another a stoneware oil lamp that looks as if it might have come out of an excavation, a very "camp" Statue of Liberty *Hanukkiah* (Hanukkah Candelabrum), and a sedate and serious needlepoint canvas. I have very deliberately set out to prove to myself (and I hope to you) that Jewish life and the Jewish holidays—in this case specifically Hanukkah—can be approached from many different points of view, that it is indeed possible to be serious at one moment and lighthearted the next. There are times when I seem to go far afield from the subject of Hanukkah, but Hanukkah means dedication, and for me it is a dedication to all of Jewish life. Hanukkah and its celebration embody for today's American Jew all of the conflicts, pressures, and pleasures of living as a Jew in a secular society.

The projects in this book should be considered as departure points, not as ends in themselves. Although I will give some step-by-step directions, my hope is that you will use these as instructions in techniques and procedures and that you will (perhaps by borrowing here and adapting there) go on to design your own work and indeed to come up with further projects—not only for Hanukkah but for the other holidays and the Jewish life cycle as well.

We are so often overwhelmed with a sense of futility, a sense of helplessness, in a world that seems to be going faster and becoming more impersonal every day. Perhaps it is helpful to keep in mind these words of Rabbi Nahman of Bratzlav: "One must repeat, from time to time: The world was created for my sake. Never say: What do I care about this or that? Do your part to add something new, to bring forth something that is needed, and to leave the world a little better because you were here briefly."

ACKNOWLEDGMENTS

Thanks to:

Dina Abromowitz and the rest of the staff at YIVO for their generous availability;

Frank J. Darmstaeder, the curator of photographs at the Jewish Theological Seminary of America, for his friendly and knowledgeable assistance;

Rabbi Hershel J. Matt for his initial encouragement and for pointing out some Hanukkah themes of which I was unaware;

Rabbi Harry Baum, for his insights and help, both practical and spiritual;

Glennis Cohen, Zelda Laschever, and Roz Staras, who I hope will recognize some of their invaluable suggestions on these pages;

Nancy Amick, Beverly Colman, Eileen Wolpert, and Frances Zeitler for helping with the sewing;

Jane Kahn, whose enthusiasm and energy were as helpful as her skills with an embroidery needle and a camera;

Yvonne Aronson and Judith Glass for the use of their ceramic studios and their expert professional advice;

Jim McDonald, for his patience and perseverence as well as his artistic and technical photographic expertise;

Peter Bedrick, of Schocken Books, for seeing the need for this book and encouraging me to do it.

Lastly, I must acknowledge the assistance of my children, David, Jeffrey, and Keren, who helped with some of the projects and were catalysts for others, who uncomplainingly (almost) endured a mother preoccupied for more than a year with *latkes* and lamps, and for whom this book is really written.

Hanukkah: Origins and Evolution

anukkah, also known as the Feast of Lights and the Festival of Dedication, is a midwinter holiday commemorating the victory of the Maccabees—Mattathias, his five sons, and their adherents—over the Syrian-Greeks, or Seleucids, in 164 B.C.E. The Syrian-Greeks had desecrated the Temple in Jerusalem, and when the triumphant Jews wrested it away from them, the Jews cleansed and rededicated it. The legend is told that when the Maccabees went to light the Temple candelabrum, only enough oil to keep it aglow for one day was found, but miraculously the oil lasted for eight days, and therefore the holiday is kept for eight days.

Since that time Hanukkah has been observed by kindling lights for eight successive days. Portions of the Torah are read in the synagogue each day of the holiday, as well as Psalms 113–118, which are hymns of praise; the prayer Al Ha-Nissim, which tells the Hanukkah story, is also recited. Work, however, continues more or less as usual, except in a few communities where women rest while the candles are burning.

For most of its history the holiday has been considered a minor one. Simple, pleasant domestic customs grew up around it, varying from country to country of the Jewish exile. During the past century, and especially since World War II, Hanukkah has grown in importance in the popular imagination. This book is a conscious attempt to grasp the reins of change as Hanukkah proceeds on its evolutionary course. If we understand the basic nature of holidays and how they grow and change, we need not deprecate our participation in the process.

THE STORY

The first Hanukkah was celebrated in Jerusalem on the twenty-fifth day of Kislev (the month in the Jewish calendar that falls roughly during November/December), 164 B.C.E. The circumstances surrounding the immediate events leading to this celebration have as many ramifications for us today as they had for the original celebrants.

A number of our holidays incorporate seasonal elements in celebration of Jewish survival in one form or another. The Passover ritual has combined two archaic nature festivals and transformed them into a commemoration of Jewish deliverance from Egyptian slavery. Purim, which also includes old seasonal customs, celebrates the legendary rescue of Persia's Jewish community through the intervention of a beautiful and brave woman; and Hanukkah, while celebrating the preservation of Judaism in the face of religious oppression, includes a reminder of ancient midwinter rites. In part, Jewish life has tenaciously persisted because of its ability to infuse the folk and nature festivals common to all people with unique historic associations, thereby giving birth to spiritual and ethical holidays that are meaningful in contemporary life.

Hanukkah is the only Jewish holiday whose historic pedigree is impeccable. To fully understand the meaning of that original Hanukkah and why the holiday is growing in importance today it is necessary to look into the ancient world and to see some of the parallels that exist between it and our life. The period of the Maccabean revolt began several years before the Temple was rededicated and extended until 140 B.C.E., when Simon, the last surviving of Mattathias' sons, was named high priest by the Great Assembly of Jerusalem and when Judea became once again an independent Jewish state—a period therefore of more than twenty-five years. Those were crucial years because it was at that time that world power was passing from Greek to Roman hands. We are accustomed to calling the classical world the Graeco-Roman world: Consider, if you will, the Judea of that time the "hyphen" as power passed from Greece to Rome. Not that Palestine was any more a bone of contention between the two great powers than any other disputed land; but at the same time the Greeks and Romans were contesting for world domination, the Jews were also trying to work out their own unique destiny. Geography kept them on the military highway as first

Greece and then Rome imposed its rule on the Middle East.

Several hundred years earlier, when Greece had defeated the Persians and briefly stopped its internal fighting under the leadership of Alexander the Great, she set out to bring Hellenic culture to the rest of the then-known world. Some historians paint Alexander as an idealist spreading truth and beauty, and perhaps in some ways he was. According to the rules of the time (and have they changed now?), winner took all. The old Persian Empire fell to Greece; in Greece it encountered the West and was hellenized. Alexander's methods were not unlike those of modern occupying forces. Trade and cultural events between the conquered people and Greece were encouraged, and many of the occupying soldiers found local girls and settled permanently in the occupied country. They married and had children, so hellenizing the population. The Jews, so the story goes, did not feel particularly threatened by the new order. They welcomed Alexander to Jerusalem with much ceremony (332 B.C.E.), declaring that they would name the male babies born in the first year of his reign Alexander; this is supposedly why there are quite a few Jewish Alexanders to this day.

About twelve years after he had built his empire, Alexander, not yet thirty-five years old, died. His enormous domain was divided up by his warring generals, Seleucis and Ptolemy, into the Seleucid (Asia Minor and Syria) and Ptolemaic (Egypt) kingdoms. Greece was left in the hands of General Antigonus. Hellenistic culture still prevailed as an elegant veneer on the former Alexandrian Empire; hellenization was either enforced or not, depending on whether Syria or Egypt had control of the area. Meanwhile, at the other end of the Mediterranean, Rome had conquered Italy and was beginning to make her presence felt.

For more than a century after the breakup of Alexander's empire Palestine was ruled by the Ptolemies of Egypt. The Ptolemaic kings collected taxes but permitted the Jews complete religious and cultural freedom and a great deal of internal self-government as well. Hellenization was not enforced but went on nevertheless. Jews learned Greek, wore the Greek tunic, and took Greek names for social, educational, and business reasons. Although to some degree almost every Jew was touched by the hellenization process, most remained true to the Mosaic faith; many also hoped for the return of Jewish kings of Davidic lineage. But living in two worlds is never easy, and the Jews found themselves internally divided between those who saw no danger in hellenization and those, more conservative, called Pietists or Hasidim*, who felt that hellenization, with its lure of pleasure and plenty, would cause the annihilation by assimilation of the Jewish people.

Thirty-four years before the Maccabean revolt, when Mattathias was a young man, the Seleucid Emperor Antiochus III of Syria concluded more than a century of political and military skirmishes and took Palestine away from the Egyptian king. Initially Antiochus III (who is the father of the Antiochus of our Hanukkah story) continued the lenient policies of the Egyptians, allowing internal self-rule as well as religious freedom to the Jews. Soon, however, he could see the glimmer of Rome on the horizon. After losing a major battle to the Romans, he decided that he could successfully defeat the Roman threat if he had a unified empire behind him, so he turned his attention to domestic politics. He began an intense program of hellenization, which included putting up statues of himself and of Greek gods in all public places—including, of course, the Temple in Jerusalem as well as synagogues throughout the land. The Jews insisted that paying taxes and fighting in the army was adequate proof of citizenship and loyalty. Antiochus III, not eager for additional internal strife, did not press the point, nor did his immediate successor and eldest son, Seleucis IV. But his second son, Antiochus IV, who next inherited the Syrian throne after the untimely death of his older brother (in which it is possible that Antiochus IV played a part), did not let the matter rest.

Antiochus IV, who called himself Antiochus Epiphanes ("god manifest") but was known among the Jews as Antiochus Epimanes ("the madman"), felt that it was a matter of principle for all the people in his realm to be totally unified. His intention was not anti-Semitic, as we understand this word today, when he insisted on the erection of statues of himself and Zeus or when he banned circumcision and Sabbath observance. He was much more like the Spanish monarchs of the fifteenth century who wanted to have a perfect Catholic land. They expelled the Jews and the Moors; anyone who remained had to convert to Catholicism. But like them and like Hitler in our own century, Antiochus became so obsessed with his monolithic idea that his political idealism became fanaticism and gave rise to intense persecution.

*The Hasidim of today, although they have the same name, do not come directly from this earlier group but rather from a group in eighteenth-century Poland which was inspired by the teachings of Israel Ben Eliezer (c. 1700–1760), known as the Baal Shem Tov.

It would be convenient to portray the ensuing twenty-five-year struggle, during which the first Hanukkah was celebrated, in the simple dramatics of a children's morality story. In this version the Syrian-Greeks are the hedonistic barbarians bearing false gods, and the Jews, pure and totally dedicated to the Torah, are united in their idealistic pursuit of religious freedom. Real life, however, is never that simple. The very complexities of the issues of that time are what continue to give Hanukkah such great meaning for us today.

As we have already seen, the process of hellenization and assimilation had been going quietly on for 125 years. When Antiochus IV announced his unification program, there were enough ardent helle-nizers of Jewish descent to enable him to appoint from among them a high priest named Jason, who in a year introduced into Jewish life more overtly Greek practices than had crept in during the entire previous century. Not only did the statues required by Antiochus' new ruling go up in the Temple, but its courtyards as well were used for Greek athletic events in which the participants were nude. Jewish priests wearing Greek clothing took part in Greek religious observances, and Jerusalem was represented by Jewish delegates at various Greek festivals. As bad as he was, Jason did come from a priestly family and did not inhibit those Jews who maintained a traditional way of life from pursuing their own practices. In short order, however, he was replaced by Menelaus, who had no family connections with the priesthood and was a rabid hellenizer.

The Hasidim, who had been disgruntled before, were now outraged. Jason, unhappy about his abrupt ouster, met with the Hasidim and planned a takeover at the first opportunity. This was not long in coming.

Antiochus, now confident that his kingdom was united behind him, set out to challenge Rome in Egypt as his father had done. Stories—fed by desire and filtered through rumor—that Antiochus had been killed in battle came to Jerusalem. The Hasidim did not wait to have the news confirmed but immediately staged a bloody massacre of Menelaus' adherents and supporters (the high priest himself was away at the time). They also destroyed the statues and other visible signs of Antiochus' power.

The rumor of Antiochus' death, however, was not true. As he was marching on Alexandria, Rome demanded that he give up his plans or face baleful consequences at the hands of the Roman legions. Antiochus

may have been arrogant, but he was not stupid; he acquiesced. Therefore, not only was he still alive, but after being so humiliated by the
Romans, he also needed a focus for his wrath and a situation in which
he could win some sort of victory. The poorly timed Hasidic revolt gave
him his opportunity and excuse. He turned his defeated army loose on
Jerusalem, where it is estimated that they killed at least ten thousand
people—Hasidim, hellenizers, and passersby. New statues were put up
in the Temple, and in order to make certain that the Jews felt the full
force of his authority, Antiochus issued decrees banning Sabbath observance, Torah study, and circumcision. Any of these were punishable by
death. Babies found to have been circumcised were hung around their
mother's necks, and both were thrown over the city walls, along with
those who had participated in the circumcision ritual.

Rather than intimidating the Jews, the indiscriminate slaughter and
the new regulations with their fierce punishments served to unit some
of the disparate segments of the Jewish community. People who had
thought of themselves as loyal Greek subjects lost members of their
family and began to identify more strongly with the Hasidim and their
cause of Jewish religious integrity. Many became martyrs, inspiring yet
more loyalty to the Jewish cause. Others, however, felt that greater
security would come by going along with the government decrees. The
Hanukkah story proper, which now begins, must be seen against this
backdrop of international politics and internal dissension.

Life in Jerusalem had turned into a nightmare. Antiochus' soldiers
patroled the streets and broke into homes, looking for anyone doing
anything recognizably Jewish. The terror that prevailed must have been
similar to that of the Spanish Inquisition. Many families fled to outlying
villages, hoping to live simple, pious lives, but Antiochus' mercenaries
pursued them there as well. The soldiers were ordered to go about the
countryside and hold official ceremonies—including the sacrifice of
pigs—in each village center to enforce recognition of Antiochus as the
divine incarnation of Zeus. As the patrols moved from village to village,
there were some cases of compliance but many more of martyrdom. An
underground literature grew up as well. Many modern scholars feel
that the books of Daniel and of Judith, and probably the story of Esther
as well, were written as inspirational and prophetic tales, portraying as
they do Jewish triumph through righteousness in the face of tyranny.

When the Syrian-Greek soldiers came to the village of Modi'in, which lies just about midway between Jerusalem and Jaffa, not far from where Lod airport is today, they met resistance of a sort they had not expected. When the soldiers tried to stage acts of pagan observance in other villages, the villagers often wouldn't cooperate, allowing themselves to be slaughtered rather than comply. In Modi'in the people turned on their oppressors and killed them.

According to the First Book of Maccabees, it happened this way: The mercenaries arrived in Modi'in with the paraphernalia necessary to perform the Greek rites. The village people were assembled, including the family of the House of Hashmon (or Hasmoneans, as we know them): Mattathias and his five sons, Johanan, Simon, Judah, Eleazar, and Jonathan.

Mattathias and his family are believed to have been among those who had chosen to leave Jerusalem rather than see it defiled. Now they were recognized as the leaders of the village. The commander of the Greek unit turned to Mattathias and said that if he would step forward to the altar, kill the sacrificial pig, and eat some of its flesh, he and his sons would be considered as Friends of the King, a title similar to a minor form of knighthood. They would also receive many royal gifts of silver and gold. Mattathias answered that neither he nor his sons nor his brothers would forsake the covenant of his fathers. "We will not obey the law of the king by departing from our worship, either to the right hand or to the left" (I Macc. 2:22).

The tension of the confrontation between the commander and Mattathias was momentarily broken by a Jew who approached the altar and declared that he would carry out the sacrificial ritual according to the king's degree. We will never know exactly what his motivations were because Mattathias was so overcome by rage that he ran forward and slew the man upon the altar itself. With the same intensity he turned upon the commander and killed him. His sons and the villagers joined in the ensuing melee and killed all the soldiers, who had most likely slackened their training, as occupying rather than combatant forces do, and so were taken by surprise.

Mattathias realized that when the patrol failed to return to headquarters, fresh troops would probably be sent to Modi'in to investigate. He, his family, and his supporters—stirred by his rallying cry, "Let everyone who is zealous for the Law and who would maintain the covenant come with me" (I Macc. 2:27)—fled to the hill country, where they could train and plan guerrilla attacks on Antiochus' soldiers.

They took with them their farm animals and as much food and basic household and farming equipment as they could, but they left the comforts of home behind. They probably also took uniforms and arms from the slain Syrian soldiers to form the nucleus of the arsenal they would need.

There has been a great deal of speculation as to exactly where they went when they fled to the mountains. We know they needed a retreat that would serve as both a hideout and a place from which they could attack. Moshe Pearlman, in his excellent political-military history *The Maccabees*, presents a convincing argument that the location chosen by the refugees was in the "hills above Gophna . . . just beyond the Judean border in southern Samaria, some 13 miles north-east of Modi'in." By looking at any map of modern Israel, one can easily locate Modi'in and form a geographical image of the places where the events we are discussing took place. Cartographers agree that because of its unique history, there have been more maps drawn of the land of Israel than of any other lump of earth. The map shown in Figure 1 is particularly interesting because it is one of the earliest views of the land to show the distribution of the various tribes. I am using it here not only for that information but also because it shows the different mountainous areas, making it easier to get a sense of the terrain on which the Hasmoneans encountered the Syrians. Modi'in, northwest of Jerusalem, is indicated by a star.

It is probable that the fugitives were not tracked down because the Syrian authorities did not expect any further trouble from them. Empires and countries frequently fell to one conquering army or another and the local population was expected to lick its wounds, pay taxes, and keep quiet. Resistance was immediately, and often brutally, squelched. By not taking them seriously, and by assuming that because the Jews of Modi'in were not recognized political figures in Jerusalem they did not pose a threat to the authorities, the Syrians made an enormous error that would lead to their eventual defeat.

Many Hasidim joined Mattathias and were eagerly accepted. In previous encounters with the Syrians a good number of Hasidim had been slaughtered in their cave hideout on the Sabbath because even when attacked, they refused to profane that day by fighting or by moving boulders to block up their caves. The Hasmoneans and their supporters decided that "if we all do as our brothers have done, and do not fight . . . for our lives and our ordinances, they will soon destroy us

from off the earth' " (I Macc. 2:40). The decision was reached to fight defensively on the Sabbath but not to initiate attacks on that day. The Hasidim went along with Mattathias in this matter, thereby recognizing his religious as well as military authority. After the Temple was regained and freedom of religious observance restored, the Hasidim once again split away from the Hasmoneans, who went on to fight for political sovereignty. The distinction between defensive and offensive action on the Sabbath has posed many problems over the centuries, and no easy solutions seem at hand even now. How bitter and reminiscent of ancient Greek techniques was the Yom Kippur attack of 1973.

The first year following the Modi'in episode was spent by the newly formed Jewish resistance principally in securing the cooperation of the local village populations and in training new recruits. They were not particularly gentle with hellenizers, since their goal was not individual freedom of religious thought as we understand it today but the strengthening and survival of a total Mosaic way of life. They did not engage in any major battles but harrassed the occupying forces by striking at patrols and disrupting the enforced Greek cultic rites.

Mattathias died during that first year and so never saw the Temple regained. Before he died he named his second son, Simon, and his third son, Judah, as his successors—Simon, because "he is a man of counsels . . . shall be a father to you. Judah Maccabee, strong and mighty from his youth, will be your captain and will fight the battle of the people" (I Macc. 2:65–66).

Even though it was Simon who, having outlived all his brothers, finally brought peace to the land and gained political independence for the country, it is Judah the Maccabee who is best remembered and glorified by history and the popular imagination, and it is by his nickname, Maccabee, that the whole group became known.

There has been a lot of discussion as to the meaning of his name. The original Hebrew spelling has been lost because the Jews did not consider the book of the Hasmonean exploits to be sacred writing. It was preserved for us in its Greek translation and only later retranslated into Hebrew. Some say it derives from the Hebrew word for "quencher," Judah having quenched Hellenism. Others maintain that it derives from the Hebrew for "hammer," because Judah dealt hammer-like blows to the Syrians, or that it signifies the fact that Judah had a head shaped like a mallet, or that it perhaps describes the personality trait of persistence. Although this last derivation seems to be the most probable, inasmuch as his father called him that before his strength in battle had really been proven, my favorite is the least likely explanation of all. According to this interpretation of the name Maccabee, Judah's battle banner was emblazoned with the phrase: מי כמוך באלים יי (*Mi kamokha ba-elim Adonai*: "Who is like unto Thee, O Lord" [Exod. 15:11, which was sung by Moses after he crossed the Red Sea.]) The letters מכבי, which spell "Maccabee," are an acrostic for this phrase.

When Judah took over after Mattathias' death, the nature of the rebels' activities changed and quickened. The third chapter of I Maccabees, which describes the major battles leading to the repossession of the Temple, opens with a powerful laudatory poem to Judah:

> And his son Judah, who was called Maccabee, rose up in his stead.
> And all his brothers helped him.
> And all those who were adherents of his father,
> And gladly they fought Israel's battle.
> He extended the glory of his people,
> And put on a breastplate as a giant,
> And girded on his weapons of war.
> He set battles in array, with the sword.
> He protected the army
> And he was like a lion in his deeds,
> And as a lion's whelp roaring for prey
> He pursued the lawless, seeking them out,
> And destroyed those who troubled his people.
> The lawless lost heart for fear of him,
> And all the workers of lawlessness were troubled;
> And deliverance prospered in his hand.
> He angered many kings,
> And made Jacob glad with his acts.
> And his memory is blessed forever.
> He went about among the cities of Judah,
> And destroyed the ungodly thereout,
> And turned away wrath from Israel.
> And he was renowned to the ends of the earth,
> And gathered together those who were perishing.
>
> —I Macc. 3:1–9

Although since leaving Modi'in their numbers had grown from forty or fifty fighters well into the thousands, the Jews were still vastly outnumbered by the Syrian mercenaries. The Syrians also had the latest weaponry at their disposal, which included ballistas (devices for throwing huge stones) and battering rams to use against walled cities as well as an abundant supply of javelins, spears, swords, bows, and protective metal armor. Their foot soldiers had battle experience and could count on assistance from cavalry and units of warrior elephants (the tanks of those days). Besides sticks and stones—which, when combined, form a mace—the Jews had only their farm animals and implements, which they converted as well as they could for military use. Whenever they could, they used captured Syrian armaments. Both sides used the shepherd's slingshot in the same manner that David used it against Goliath.

Newspaper coverage of the Viet Nam war in recent years has shown us how time and again the Viet Cong guerrillas could strike devastating blows against "superior" forces because they could fade into friendly villages and count on food and shelter until it was time to strike again. It was precisely this advantage that Judah and his men exploited against a huge, well-trained, and well-equipped army. The militia system they set up probably differed only in details from the citizens' army of modern Israel. There were too many of the new recruits for all of them to hide in the mountains. Feeding them would have been impossible. It is likely that after training they would return to their homes and continue farming or practicing whatever other occupation they had, thereby serving as links in the intelligence and communication network that was as essential to the conduct of warfare then as it is today. When they were needed, they were called by the local commander.

There were four major battles against the Syrians before the Temple was regained. The Maccabees won decisive victories in the face of overwhelming odds because, in the words of encouragement Judah gave his men, "Victory in battle does not depend on the size of an army, but strength is from Heaven. They are advancing against us, full of violence and lawlessness, to destroy us and our wives and our children, and to plunder us. We are fighting for our lives and our Laws. And He Himself will shatter them before us; but as for you, be not afraid of them" (I Macc. 3:19–22).

The occupation government couldn't ignore the rebel activities forever. As Judah's men grew in numbers, strength, and experience, they staged more frequent harrassing skirmishes. Finally General Apollonius marched on Judah's stronghold with a large army from Samaria. Judah and his men ambushed them en route. Apollonius and many of his men were killed; those who weren't, fled. Judah's rebel band gathered up the weapons and armor of their defeated enemy for future use; Judah used Apollonius' sword in battle for the rest of his life.

When news of Apollonius' defeat reached Syria, General Seron decided to build his reputation by defending the king's law and taking revenge on the Jews. It would have been faster for him to move directly south toward Judea, but he decided instead to stick to the long coastal road, turning inland at Jaffa. His army is estimated to have been at least twice the size of Apollonius'. After turning east at Jaffa, he was set upon at the Beth Horon pass in the mountains about twelve miles northwest of Jerusalem. Judah and some of his men had been watching the Syrian troops approach; they descended upon the mercenaries and chased them down the hills from Beth Horon as far as the coastal plain. About eight hundred men were killed.

Rather than enhance the reputation of General Seron, this encounter served to spread the fame of Judah and to attract even more supporters to his cause. When King Antiochus heard of this, he was furious. He wasn't about to abandon plans he had already made to travel to Persia to collect revenue with which to support his luxurious habits; but before leaving, he entrusted half his army and elephants to Lysias, a man so much in his confidence that he left him his son to raise as well. He had perfect faith that Lysias would do everything necessary to "destroy the strength of Israel and the remnant of Jerusalem, and to remove their memory from the place [and to] make strangers to dwell in all their borders, and [to] divide their land by lot" (I Macc. 3:35–36).

Lysias left nothing to chance. He appointed two high-ranking generals, Gorgias and Nicanor, to head the campaign against the Maccabees. Between them they commanded about twenty thousand foot soldiers and cavalry. Like Seron, they proceeded down the coast road, but in order to avoid being pounced upon in the mountains as Seron had been, they set up their camp on the Judean plain near the town of Emmaus, about fifteen miles northwest of Jerusalem. The plains would give the Syrian troops and cavalry, which were accustomed to fighting in fixed formations, more room to maneuver than would the hill country, which was better suited to the needs of the guerrilla fighters.

So confident were they of victory that they attracted slave dealers who joined them in anticipation of buying up the defeated Jews.

The odds were awesome, but fortified with prayer and Judah's words—"It is better for us to die in battle than to look upon the evils that have come upon our nation and our sanctuary" (I Macc. 3:59)—the Maccabees staged several brilliant maneuvers and crushed the Syrian forces, driving the survivors back up the coast road. When the bedraggled survivors of Nicanor's and Gorgias' armies reached Syria with the news of their staggering defeat, Antiochus' trusted deputy, Lysias, resolved to take matters completely into his own hands and to lead the next onslaught against Judea himself. This he did the following spring. With at least twenty thousand men and three to four thousand cavalry he determined to attack Judea from the south. He followed the same coastal road from Syria as his predecessors had, but this time he went farther south, heading east about the latitude of Ashkalon; he thus kept in territory friendly to himself and avoided being attacked en route. He set up camp at Beth Zur in southern Judea, about twenty miles southwest of Jerusalem on the road from Hebron. The land there is very hilly, and therefore, even though Judah and his ten thousand men were outnumbered, they were able to use the landscape to their advantage. In the close quarters of the mountainous terrain Judah's men killed five thousand of Lysias' mercenaries; others began to desert. When Lysias saw the intensity with which the Maccabees fought, he ordered a retreat and departed for Antioch, the Syrian capital. There he enlisted even more soldiers, with the intention of returning to Judea.

Although this important victory did not end the hostilities, it did mark the beginning of the celebration of Hanukkah. For the Maccabees, even though they knew that Lysias would attack again, this was an hour of triumph. There was still a Syrian garrison entrenched in Jerusalem, but flushed with their victory over Lysias' army, they marched up to the holy city. Judah dispatched some troops to fight off the enemy soldiers stationed there and went to the Temple to cleanse and rededicate it.

"They saw the sanctuary laid desolate, and the altar profaned, and the gates burned up, and weeds growing in the courts as in a forest or upon one of the mountains, and the chambers pulled down; and they rent their garments, and made great lamentations, and put ashes on their heads; and they fell on their faces to the ground, and they blew the solemn blasts upon the trumpets, and cried unto Heaven" (I Macc.

4:38–40). Then they set to work to clear away the debris and remainders of Greek cultic use, rebuilding wherever necessary.

> They took whole stones, according to the Law, and built a new altar after the fashion of the former; and they built the sanctuary, and the inner parts of the Temple, and hallowed the courts. And they made the holy vessels new, and they brought the candlestick, the altar of burnt offerings and of incense, and the table, into the Temple. And they burned incense upon the altar, and they lit the lamps that were upon the candlestick in order to give light in the Temple. And they set loaves upon the table, and hung up the curtains, and finished all the works which they had undertaken. . . . And they rose up early in the morning on the twenty-fifth of . . . Kislev [three years after Antiochus had desecrated the Temple] . . . . At the corresponding time and on the corresponding day on which the gentiles had profaned it, on that very day it was dedicated afresh, with songs and harps and lutes, and with cymbals. . . . They celebrated the dedication of the altar for eight days, and offered burnt offerings with gladness, and sacrificed a sacrifice of deliverance and praise. And they decked the front of the Temple with crowns of gold and small shields, and dedicated afresh the gates and the chambers, and furnished them with doors. . . . Judah and his brothers and the whole congregation of Israel ordained that the days of the dedication of the altar should be kept in their season year by year for eight days, from the twenty-fifth of the month Kislev, with gladness and joy [I Macc. 4:47–60].

Looking at the original Hanukkah celebration as it is recorded in the First Book of Maccabees gives an intense feeling of immediacy to the event. In designing the projects for this book I have tried to cut through all the intervening centuries (stopping off for occasional inspiration along the way) in order to establish a more direct link between what happened then and twentieth-century Jewish life. Some historical parallels are as evident as they are painful: "When the gentiles around them heard that the altar had been built and the sanctuary dedicated as before, they became angry. And they determined to destroy the descendants of Jacob who were among them, and began to slay and to destroy among the people" (I Macc. 5:1–2). And so at the same time that Judah and his men celebrated the first Hanukkah, "they built high walls and strong towers around Mount Zion, so that the gentiles could

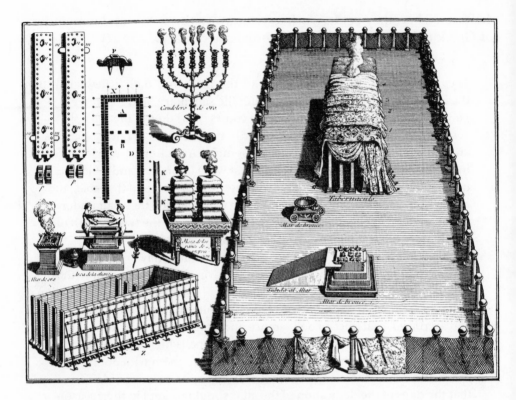

2 This engraving from an eighteenth-century Dutch book depicts the Temple furniture, including the seven-branched golden menorah, the table for shew-bread, the sacrifical altar, and the Ark of the Covenant.

never again come and destroy them, as they had done before'' (I Macc. 4:60–61).

The Temple was purified, but the fighting went on for several more years, until Lysias annulled the anti-Jewish decrees and the Jews were officially granted the religious freedom they had fought so hard to attain. At this point many of the Hasidim, their goal achieved, dropped out of the fighting. The Maccabees, however, were not to be satisfied until they had gained political independence as well. It took almost twenty more years for the last Syrian troops to be forced from Jerusalem and for Judea again to be—after the more than four hundred years since the Babylonian exile—a sovereign nation. Simon, "the man of counsels" and now the only surviving Maccabee, was proclaimed high priest by the Great Assembly, and as commander and ruler he established the Hasmonean dynasty. He concluded a treaty of friendship with Rome, by then clearly the dominant world power. The men from Modi'in could never have dreamed that their people would be driven from the land by these very Romar∋, to live as strangers for almost two thousands years until, in our own age, Israel is once again an independent state.

Is it any wonder then that Hanukkah, which couples the spirit of religious freedom with national integrity, has over the last century, and particularly the latter decades of it, come to be a holiday that all Jews in a secular age can celebrate with emotional intensity approaching the religious fervor of previous eras?

THE HOLIDAY

The history of a holiday's observance can be as fascinating as the history of the event being commemorated. Jews have celebrated Hanukkah for twenty-one centuries.

To the casual observer it might seem that the nature of Hanukkah observance has changed solely in response to the pervasiveness of the Christmas mentality in American life. It cannot be denied that in every society in which Jews have lived, their contact with neighboring cultures has presented challenges to the concept of separateness so ingrained in Jewish thought. As we have seen, the very struggle of the Maccabees was in part a civil war between those Jewish elements who saw in the splendors of the material culture of Greece and Hellenism the gateway to a better life—the answer to the Jewish problem of being the outsider—and Jewish traditionalists, who felt that only by the total rejection of Hellenism would Judaism maintain its integrity and historic mission. In those days the Greeks sent scouts to all the outlying provinces to look for talent for their many cultural undertakings. Much as baseball and football scouts scour the minor leagues, looking for next year's hero, the Greeks came to the towns of Judea in search of the best young athletes to participate in the arenas of Greece. Greek athletes competed in the nude, and only the "perfect and complete" body was acceptable. Many young Jews therefore underwent a very painful operation to erase the traces of their circumcision in order to qualify for the Greek games. The lure of the stranger has been with us for a very long time. Although it would be easier to say that the resurgence of interest in Hanukkah is due only to the provocation of Christmas, I feel that it is necessary to search a bit deeper and to realize how the changing circumstances of Jewish life itself have made it opportune for certain qualities that have always been implicit in Hanukkah to now become explicit.

The major Jewish holidays were not always as important as we know them today, and conversely some of the minor holidays were once of greater significance. The crucible of time and events gave greater importance to one or the other, and often, as one holiday was observed with greater intensity, another was fading into obscurity. The Fast of Esther, which precedes Purim, was for the Marranos during the period of the Inquisition more significant than Yom Kippur. The Marranos identified with the plight of Esther as a stranger in a foreign court, and because little attention was paid to the Fast of Esther, they could observe it with less danger of being denounced to the Inquisition. For many centuries Rosh Hodesh (the Festival of the New Moon) was observed as a significant holiday, particularly by women. Today, except for the more observant, many Jews are not even familiar with the name of the holiday, much less with its rituals. There has been some speculation that since feminism is rising among Jewish women, Rosh Hodesh, with its very female lunar associations, will once again regain its popularity.

All holidays have their origins in nature and the seasonal changes, and people throughout the world celebrate similar festivals at roughly the same time throughout the year. The meaning and interpretation they give to their respective holy days depend on particular events in the history of the group and its particular needs. Thus for the Jews ancient Middle Eastern fire-lighting winter rites became associated with the events that occurred in Judea in the second century B.C.E.

As described in the First Book of Maccabees, the first Hanukkah celebrated by Judah and his men was inaugurated as a holiday of rededication of the Temple. It was ordained then that the holiday should be kept joyously for eight days at the appropriate season. In the Second Book of Maccabees (which was probably written some twenty years after I Maccabees and, while sticking to the same historic events, includes additional episodes of martyrdom), Hanukkah is described as a second Sukkot as well as a festival of rededication. As at Sukkot, the *lulav* (palm branch) was waved, and *Hallel* (psalms of thanksgiving and praise) were sung. The reason given is that the people had been fugitives not long before; thus when it was time to celebrate Sukkot, they had not been able to observe the holiday properly, although they had been living in the customary temporary dwellings. Having Sukkot in Kislev would recompense them for what they had missed.

An attractive legend arose to explain the reason for celebrating Hanukkah for eight days: When the Maccabees reclaimed the Temple, they found eight Syrian spears, which they converted into a lamp stand. It is more likely, however, that the early identification of Sukkot with the new holiday explains the eight days of celebration, as well as the inclusion of *Hallel* in the daily service throughout the holiday. Though it began in part as a second Sukkot—and some of that holiday's attributes still cling to it—the fact that it celebrates the rededication of the Temple and of the human spirit, has given Hanukkah its unique character. The holiday has links with older dedication observances. When Moses built the Tabernacle in the desert, he had a dedication ceremony. Solomon had a similar service when the first Temple was built, and the Jews who returned from the Babylonian Exile had a dedication service when they built the Second Temple. As a religious commemoration, the holiday therefore followed historical precedent.

What made Hanukkah difficult to celebrate, if not downright dangerous, was its definite military-political overtones. By the time the Hasmonean dynasty was established, Rome was the ascendant world power. We have little information about the nature of Hanukkah observance during the brief century of Hasmonean independence, but we know that under Roman rule the Jews were once again denied political and religious freedom. Once Judea had lost the last crumb of autonomy, Jews were in no position to celebrate a holiday with so much nationalistic content.

Nevertheless, the holiday survived. For twenty-one centuries, in the many lands of the Diaspora as well as in Israel, the Hanukkah flames have been lit as a commemoration of the miracle that occurred in ancient Judea. As we will see in the next chapter, Talmudic legend provided a more romantic and less threatening miracle than the real one of the tenacious persistence of Jewish faith; indeed, I know of nothing more miraculous than the survival, both physical and spiritual, of the Jewish people.

After the year 70 C.E., when the Temple was destroyed, and after the heroic last stand of the defenders of Massadah in 73 and the Bar Kokhba rebellion (132–135), Hanukkah was observed as a holiday of rededication of the Temple and of the religious spirit; its nationalistic aspects were muted. Later, wherever the Jews lived in exile, they were strangers, and even if they were accepted into the life of the host country, their privileges could be extinguished as quickly as a candle flame at the whim of those in power. In the third century C.E. fire was considered sacred in Persia, and the kindling of Hanukkah lights was banned. In the Middle Ages the continuity of Jewish values and thought in Europe was taken for granted: Assimilation wasn't a danger; it was an impossibility. Rather, the threat to Jewish life was physical and came from the outside. This may be one of the reasons for the popularity of Purim during those years. Hanukkah celebrates the rescue of Judaism itself from annihilation; Purim, which coincides with the Christian carnival period, celebrates the *physical* rescue of the Jews of Persia through the intervention of Queen Esther and therefore reflects the concerns of Jewish life in the Middle Ages as well as later, in the villages of the Pale of Settlement.

In our century fully one third of the world's Jewish population was slaughtered, and Israel was reborn as a nation. In Israel, where secularism has touched the Jews as it has in this country, Hanukkah is the holiday that every Israeli celebrates with a full heart. Israeli soldiers—and everyone in Israel is a soldier—are likened to the Maccabees, and Hanukkah lights are kindled at Modi'in as well as on the heights of Massadah. When the Ashkenazic Chief Rabbi Shlomo Goren lit the first wick of the oil-burning *hanukkiah* at the Western Wall in Jerusalem in 1974, he said: "Let us remember our ancestors, the Hasmoneans, who never put down their weapons nor gave up their faith. May we recapture their spirit, and thereby merit a true peace in our own day. Let us remember the innocent people who died by the hand of terrorists, and our soldiers who fell in the struggle for freedom and independence in the Land of Israel" (*Jerusalem Post*, December 10, 1974).

In America, however, many people feel that Hanukkah is being inflated in order to compete with Christmas. I cannot deny that there may be some truth in this charge. The culture does put incredible pressure on parents to *do something* for their Santa-starved offspring. We must realize, however, that if America did not give us the constitutional right of religious freedom, Christmas could have the very opposite effect. It is, unfortunately (and contrary, I feel, to the First Amendment), a national holiday, but it is not obligatory to observe it, nor is it forbidden to ignore it and go about one's own holiday business. Thus in

America Jews have unique conditions for religious self-expression which they have seldom had elsewhere.

Other special conditions here combine with religious freedom to give impetus to the development of Hanukkah into a major celebration. Like most of my generation, I grew up with the vision of America as a melting pot. All the different nationalities would come together in America and simmer down within a few generations into an easily digestible puree. It seems that some of the lumps refused to melt, and now some cultural historians are using the image of a salad bowl rather than a melting pot to describe our pluralistic society. In recent years we have witnessed an intense revival of ethnic consciousness among all groups. Just a few years ago a new holiday began in the black communities of California. Now nationwide, it is called Kwanza and incorporates many familiar agricultural and midwinter rites, such as candle-lighting. The holiday is based on African harvest celebrations (the name means "first fruits" in Swahili) and is celebrated for seven days, from December 26 to January 1, promoting "unity in the family, the community, the nation, and the race."

American Jews don't have to formulate a holiday to celebrate their sense of identification with their people. Hanukkah has been waiting for centuries. It is now being brought out and dusted off a little. With the blanket approval afforded by the Constitution, the impetus of the ethnic revival, and the close ties Jews here feel with Israel—both the land and the people—Hanukkah is ready to grow and fill the need of today's Jews for a holiday expressing dedication to a people and a nation as well as to a religious belief.

There are awkward moments as Hanukkah makes the transition into a major holiday. In the late 1950s there was a short-lived vogue for "Hanukkah bushes" decorated in blue and white. As we become more comfortable with some of Hanukkah's Americanized styling, it is to be hoped that we will make the most of our American freedoms, exercising good taste and judgment to produce a holiday atmosphere that illuminates our contemporary spiritual needs at the same time as we pay homage to the heroism and martyrdom of past centuries.

Lights

THE STORY

T he main feature of the celebration of Hanukkah is the kindling of
lights on the eight successive nights of the holiday. It is curious that
this one universal ceremonial act has in fact nothing to do with the
historical origins of Hanukkah. When we were children we were
told that when Judah and his men rededicated the Temple and were
about to kindle the menorah, they found buried in the debris left by
Antiochus a small cruse of unprofaned oil which had been closed with
the seal of the high priest and hidden away in the days of the Prophet
Samuel (c. 1100–1020 B.C.E.). Samuel, who anointed Saul as first king of
Israel, has been endowed in Jewish folklore with the ability to bring on
rain through the saintliness of his prayers and his life. It is no surprise,
then, that the tiny vessel of oil, supposedly dating from Samuel's
lifetime, which the Maccabees "found" and which contained only
enough oil for one day, should miraculously burn for eight days until
new clean oil was obtained. Thus the miracle of the oil often becomes
the explanation for the holiday and for its duration of eight days.

This is a lovely legend, but by the time we have come to understand
the struggle between Hellenism and Hebraism, with the ultimate victory of the Maccabees as the basis for the holiday, we know as we
kindle the Hanukkah lights that the miracle of the oil is a poetic
substitution for the miracle of Jewish survival. The flames reflect the
glow of the religious freedom the Maccabees fought for.

If the story of the oil is only a folktale, why then do we light flames
on Hanukkah? It is this question which the authors of the Talmud were

23

3 Placing the Hanukkah lamp in the window tells passersby which night of the holiday it is by the number of candles in the lamp as it "proclaims the miracle."

trying to answer in the second century C.E. when they asked, "What is Hanukkah?" (Shabbat 21b). The holiday is touched on only incidentally in the Talmud, in the section about the proper oil to use for the Sabbath lights. Hanukkah lamps then come under discussion and the story of the miraculous cruse of oil is told in explanation of the lighting of Hanukkah lamps. The story thus can be said to have been invented in order to give a Jewish explanation for a practice that was already entrenched among the people.

Historians suggest a variety of derivations for the Hanukkah lights, including Greek revelries associated with Dionysus, the mythological god of wine and drama, and Syrian celebrations of the winter solstice. On the other hand, much modern scholarship now holds that the lights did not arise from any such non-Jewish ceremonies. We need not enter these debates when we acknowledge that for as long as the land we know as Eretz Israel has been inhabited, fires have been lit during that time of year when the nights are longest and the periods of light and warmth shortest. In earliest times people, feeling helpless in the cold and dark of winter, sought to relume the sun and bring it back to life by lighting huge ceremonial fires. Obviously it worked; the sun came back. Thus reinforced with success, the custom became firmly rooted, and every winter fires were lit and appropriate chants recited. The arguments are often raised that Jews follow a lunar calendar and therefore couldn't possibly observe a festival associated with a solar phenomenon and that if the Maccabees were fighting for religious separatism, they would not institute a holiday based on Grecian rites. These would be valid objections if people were totally rational and holidays came about in the simple, orderly manner that is most conveniently used to explain their origins.

Holidays change their meanings but not their seasons. We do not know with total accuracy what type of winter folk customs the Jews observed at the time of the Maccabean revolt. Only the religious observances that were officially sanctioned have been documented for us. Alongside these, folk beliefs and customs undoubtedly flourished. In the First Book of Maccabees we read that when Judah rededicated the Temple, he lit the Temple lamp stand. When the Temple stood, the menorah was lit all the time, and by relighting it, Judah was reestablishing the usual practice. No mention was made in the early writings of a miraculous cruse of oil.

A number of different Jewish holidays originated during the Hasmonean period. One, called Nicanor Day, celebrated Judah's victory over a General Nicanor. We don't know very much about this holiday, but unlike Hanukkah, it totally disappeared from Jewish life. If, like Nicanor Day, Hanukkah had been only a holiday to commemorate military exploits, it is probable that it too would have disappeared. Although in this century the military and nationalistic aspects of Hanukkah are again surfacing, it is the spiritual meaning of Hanukkah which has kept it a living holiday these many centuries and which provides its universal meaning even in today's secular world. The

Maccabees fought first for religious freedom and only later for political independence. Since at that time religion was a total spiritual-economic-political package, the fight for national sovereignty was but a continuation of the struggle for religious autonomy.

Since their earliest history the Jews have identified light with holiness and the Divine Presence and have ritualized its use in the celebration of major holidays and events in the cycle of life. The kindling of lights both initiates and terminates the Sabbath. Passover, Shavuot, Rosh Hashonah, Yom Kippur, Sukkot, and Shemini Atzeret (the last day of Sukkot before Simhat Torah) are all begun with the kindling of lights. Twenty-four-hour candles are burned for the first seven days after the death of a family member, on the anniversary of his or her death, and again to honor his or her memory on Yom Kippur. Every synogogue has a *Ner Tamid* (an Eternal Light) near the Ark of the Law. Yom ha-Shoah (Martyrs' Day), a new holiday still in the formative stages, coming after Passover and before Israeli Independence Day, is observed by some by burning a *yahrzeit* (anniversary) candle placed in a window in memory of the six million victims of the Holocaust. If by lighting fires at Hanukkah time the Jews were appropriating and adapting customs of surrounding peoples, this came about within the framework of the ancient (even at that time) internal history of symbolic use of sacramental fire. Since from its inception Hanukkah meant more than simple rejoicing at a military victory, a suitable soul-stirring ritual was necessary to perpetuate its religious meanings, and lighting flames provided this. Therefore it should not surprise us that the original Sukkot type of observances with which the Maccabees celebrated their victory should, in the centuries immediately following the Hasmonean rule, fall away and that the new-old one of midwinter fire-lighting —with its profound spiritual (as well as superstitious) overtones— should replace them as the means of commemorating the Maccabean struggle for religious freedom.

When the Talmud was being compiled, its authors chose to ignore the military victories of the Maccabees and to emphasize the spiritual triumphs. It was obvious to them (Rome had already destroyed the Temple regained by Judah) that physical power is more ephemeral than the strength of the spirit. So in their rhetorical response to the question "What is Hanukkah?" they discussed and codified the manner in which Hanukkah was celebrated, not the historical events that brought it into being. Legends are as revealing as history for the understanding of holidays. History tells us more or less what happened; legend explains what we feel about what happened. So for all these hundreds of years we have kindled the Hanukkah lights, grateful for a miracle as multi-faceted as a flame.

By deliberately and carefully prescribing the manner and circumstances of kindling the Hanukkah lights, the early sages sought to break whatever links might remain between Jewish custom and those of neighboring cultures. Thus, no matter what form a Hanukkah lamp may take, it is essential that the flames remain separate and not blend to resemble a pagan bonfire. Since no single day of Hanukkah is more important than any other, traditional Hanukkah lamps are designed so that all of the lights are on the same level. Only the *shammash* may be higher. However, many contemporary lamps have been made without regard for this custom.

Originally the lights were kindled in the streets outside the house, supposedly because Antiochus had forced the people to have pagan altars in front of their homes and so having Hanukkah lights there obliterated the former profanation. Having the lights outside also served to proclaim the miracle. Their exposure to the inclement winter weather must have made it necessary to enclose them in some sort of lantern. The custom then grew up of hanging the lamp on the entrance doorpost, opposite the mezuzah. In that way it would be shielded from weather but still proclaim the commemorated events. If a person lives in the upper story of a building, the precept is fulfilled by placing the lamp in a window. This is now the custom common even among those with easy access to front entrances. In times of persecution or danger, the lamp can be placed on an interior table away from the gaze of hostile parties.

There was a debate, finally resolved in the first century C.E., as to whether eight lights should be kindled on the first night and their number diminished with each subsequent evening of the holiday or whether the number of lights should increase. As we know, the latter view, expounded by the school of Hillel—that gladness and joy should increase with each day of the holiday—prevailed over the more austere opinion of the school of Shammai. Originally oil lamps were used, and they are still widely used among many Oriental and Sephardic communities, but wax candles are more common today. Just as Hebrew is read from right to left, the candles are placed in the *hanukkiah* beginning at the right side and increasing daily toward the left. The most recently added candle is lit first, using a servant candle called the *shammash*. The *shammash* is used because the Hanukkah lights are holy and not to be used for illumination or to kindle another flame. The candles or oil wicks should last for at least half an hour. Every Hanukkah will include at least one Shabbat. The Hanukkah lights are kindled before lighting the Sabbath candles on Friday night. If Havdalah (the ceremony connoting the differentiation between the holiness of the Sabbath day and the ordinary days of the week) is said at home, it precedes the lighting of the Hanukkah candles; in the synagogue, Havdalah is said after the Hanukkah lights are kindled.

Hanukkah, which began as a Temple observance, shortly developed into a warm domestic celebration. Since the destruction of the Temple by the Romans in 70 C.E., the family table has in many ways become an altar and the family its officiants. The candles can be lit any time after sunset; a good time to do so is immediately before sitting down to dinner, when the entire family is gathered. Whether you have a lamp for each member of the household or all share one, it is especially meaningful for everyone—men, women, and children—to have a chance to kindle at least one light during the course of the holiday. The miracle was for all of us.

First the *shammash* is lit; but before using it to kindle the other lights, the following blessings are recited:

Barukh atah adonai elohenu melekh ha-olam　　ברוך אתה יי אלהינו מלך העולם
asher kiddshanu bemitzvatav vetzivanu　　　　אשר קדשנו במצותיו וצונו
lehadlik ner shel Hanukkah.　　　　　　　　　להדליק נר של חנוכה

Blessed are You, O Lord, our God,
King of the Universe, who sanctified us
with His commandments and commanded us to kindle the Hanukkah
lights.

Barukh atah adonai elohenu melekh ha-olam　　ברוך אתה יי אלהינו מלך העולם
she-asa nissim la-avotenu bayyamim hahem　　שעשה נסים לאבותינו בימים ההם
bazzman hazzeh.　　　　　　　　　　　　　　בזמן הזה

Blessed are You, O Lord, our God,
King of the Universe, who performed
miracles for our ancestors in days gone
by at this season of the year.

Barukh atah adonai elohenu melekh ha-olam
shehecheyanu vekimanu vehigiyanu
lazzman hazzeh.

ברוך אתה יי אלהינו מלך העולם
שהחינו וקימנו והגיענו
לזמן הזה.

Blessed are You, O Lord, our God,
King of the Universe, who has kept us
in life and enabled us to reach this day.

The last of these three prayers, the *Shehecheyanu* prayer, is said only on the first night. This prayer is also recited at the beginning of every festival and on special occasions such as a Bar Mitzvah or wedding and when moving into a new home, getting new clothes, or tasting a seasonal fruit for the first time in the year. After the candles are lit and the *shammash* replaced in the lamp, it is customary to recite or chant the following:

הנרות הללו אנחנו מדליקין על הנסים ועל התשועות ועל הנפלאות
שעשית לאבותינו על־ידי כהניך הקדושים; וכל־שמונת ימי חנוכה
הנרות הללו קדש ואין לנו רשות להשתמש בהם, אלא לראותם בלבד,
כדי להודות לשמך על־נסיך ועל ישועתך ועל־נפלאותיך.

We kindle these lights on account of the miracles, the deliver-
ances, and the wonders You performed for our fathers, by
means of Your holy priests. During all the eight days of Hanukkah these lights are sacred, and it is not permitted for us to make
any use of them, but only to look at them, in order that we may
give thanks unto Your Name for Your miracles, Your deliver-
ances, and Your wonders.

Among Sephardim the Thirtieth Psalm is then recited. This is a psalm attributed to King David which is also called "A Song at the Dedication of the House." It has been suggested that it was chanted by Judah and his men when they rededicated the Temple. Ashkenazim rarely recite it at home but do so at synagogue services for Hanukkah. "Maoz Tzur" ("Rock of Ages") is usually sung by Ashkenazim after the candle-lighting ceremony. The verses of this hymn were composed in the Middle Ages by a man named Mordecai, who "signed" his work by using the letters of his name to begin each verse, thereby forming an acrostic. At one time it was sung to a different melody than the one now familiar, which is a combination of a sixteenth-century German church hymn and a German folk melody.

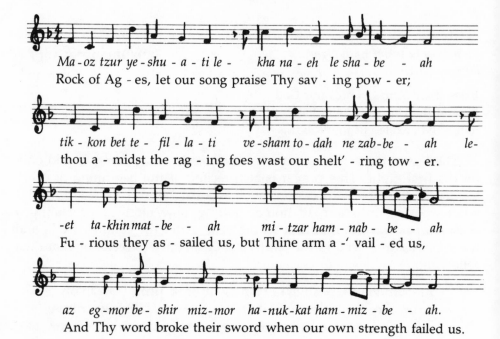

Ma - oz tzur ye - shu - a - ti le - kha na - eh le sha - be - ah
Rock of Ag - es, let our song praise Thy sav - ing pow - er;

tik - kon bet te - fil - la - ti ve - sham to - dah ne zab - be - ah le-
thou a - midst the rag - ing foes wast our shelt' - ring tow - er.

-et ta - khin mat - be - ah mi - tzar ham - nab - be - ah
Fu - rious they as - sailed us, but Thine arm a -' vail - ed us,

az eg - mor be - shir miz - mor ha - nuk - kat ham - miz - be - ah.
And Thy word broke their sword when our own strength failed us.

In Hebrew "Maoz Tzur" is a song of praise for the rededication of the Temple.

THE LAMPS

Confusion exists in the minds of many people between the seven-branched menorah and the nine-branched lamp, the *hanukkiah*, which is used during the Hanukkah celebration. There are two religiously significant Jewish candelabra. The menorah, with its treelike form symbolically combining heavenly light and earthly strength, is the more ancient of the two lamps. According to Exodus 37:17 *ff.*, the first one was made from a solid block of gold for the desert Tabernacle by the divinely inspired Bezalel. Eventually this candelabrum was installed in Solomon's Temple. When Judah and his men rededicated the Temple, the lamp they lit was a seven-branched menorah, probably a copy of Bezalel's original, which may very well have been lost or melted down as a result of one of the periodic Temple sackings.

Both because of the nature of the holiday and because it is forbidden to reproduce the Temple menorah, the *hanukkiah* followed its own course of development, producing a unique body of religious art objects. Although the menorah was from the very beginning used as a decorative symbol on *hanukkiot* (as well as on tombstones, manuscripts,

4 Four antique lamps, variously from (starting from the top, clockwise) Spanish Morocco, Poland, Israel, and Poland.

etc.), it was not until the Middle Ages that menorah-form Hanukkah lamps were made. A tree of life aglow with divine light is too powerful a symbol to be indefinitely confined to two dimensions, and it was reasoned that since the Hanukkah lamp had nine branches and the size, material, and mode of decoration was so different from the Temple original, it was no longer considered a transgression to make *hanukkiot* of the menorah type. These days the general confusion is compounded because the word "menorah" is often used as a general term to identify either lamp.

It is believed that the earliest lamps used for Hanukkah were the simple pear-shaped ceramic oil lamps common throughout the Mediterranean world, such as the one shown in the foreground of Figure 4, which was found in an excavation in Israel. These were probably lined up on a pedestal in front of the house, an additional lamp added each night until the total of eight was reached. It is conjectured that a pitcher-shaped lamp was used as the *shammash*. Contemporary photographs of Jews from Bukhara show them lighting Hanukkah candles set on the bottoms of inverted Oriental handleless teacups arranged in a line. The place for the *shammash* was made by placing the inverted teacup over a rice bowl, thereby raising it above the other candles. My mother told me that she and her brother had once lined up potato halves to use as a Hanukkah lamp when they were refugees in Poland during World War I.

Children are intrigued with the idea of making things with rearrangeable parts. The *hanukkiah* in Figure 5 was made by my daughter when she was seven years old. She had at the time been making little lions from clay and plasticine in her school art class, so she knew just how she wanted to make her candleholders. She had always liked to draw elephants but had never made a three-dimensional one. I showed her some illustrations of the warrior elephants used by the Syrians against the Maccabees and that determined what her *shammash* would look like. The elephant has often been used as a symbol for Hanukkah, for despite its use by the enemy, the Jews were victorious. The Jewish Museum in New York City has in its superb collection of Hanukkah

5 Ceramic lions and a warrior elephant form a Hanukkah caravan. From year to year the candlesticks have also been arranged in circles, pairs, or arcs—whichever suited the mood of the moment.

lamps a silver one from India which has the *shammash* light held by a man sitting on an elephant.

Adults as well as children like to work with clay. With the renaissance of home crafts there is scarcely a community in America without some facilities where you can fire your ceramics. If you are already involved in ceramic activities, perhaps this book will offer some new ideas to try; if on the other hand you have never worked with clay but would like to, my first suggestion is to find out where in your local area you can have your work fired. Many artist-ceramicists as well as semi-commercial kilns rent space at so much per square inch. Look in the Yellow Pages and ask lots of questions at local galleries and craft fairs. The types of clay and glaze you use will depend on the kiln that is available to you. The ceramist in charge of the kiln will probably be able to tell you where to get materials. Look through some basic ceramic technique books in the library; the children's section will probably give you more than enough information to begin. (After you have become addicted is time enough to read advanced technical material.)

Except for the elephant banks (page 67) and two of the plates (pages 88 and 91), all the ceramic projects in this book were made without a wheel, using the simple, direct method of cutting and folding rolled-out slabs of clay into the desired shapes. Sometimes two or more slabs were joined together, much as a dressmaker or carpenter joins objects by means of a seam, using clay mixed with vinegar (slip) as the adhesive. The lamp at the beginning of this chapter (Figure 3), the elephant and lions in Figure 5, and the chessmen in Figure 56 were made by the "pinch and squeeze" method we all permitted ourselves to enjoy when we were children on the beach or playing with plasticine—that is, by simply using the fingers to mold the pieces into the desired shapes and configurations.

Once you have arranged for firing the pieces and have the materials on hand, all that you must remember is: Wedge (knead) the clay thoroughly to be certain all the air bubbles are out (so your work won't explode in the kiln when the trapped air expands in the heat). Keep the work damp, under plastic sheets or bags, between work sessions. Let everything dry very slowly (this is especially important for hand-built pieces with many joints) to avoid cracks. Be bold and deliberate as you handle the clay—hesitancy and overwork show. If you are having a good time, that shows too.

Depressions were made in the elephant's and lions' backs while the clay was still wet to accommodate the candles they would later hold. Since clay shrinks during drying and firing, remember to make the candleholders larger than you will need them.

Oil Lamps

In spite of all the years I had heard and told the story of the legendary cruse of oil and in spite of the fact that I have collected both old and new oil lamps, I had never tried lighting an oil lamp until I undertook the writing of this book. It really is fun, and I heartily recommend it. If you have trouble acquiring an oil-burning lamp and finding adequate wicking, do not despair; both problems can be handled with a little work and ingenuity.

Directions for two oil-burning lamps follow. One is for those readers who have access to ceramic facilities; the other can be assembled in an afternoon from readily available materials.

One of the oldest lamps thought to have been made especially for Hanukkah was unearthed in Israel and is believed to be from the Talmudic period (first to second centuries C.E.). It is a ceramic eight-spouted *polymixos* with an additional large orifice into which the oil is poured.* Erwin R. Goodenough, in his exhaustive study, *Jewish Symbols in the Graeco-Roman Period*, also reproduces several such lamps, so they must have been typical of the period. This lamp probably developed from the pear-shaped prototype discussed earlier. A number of them bearing symbols depicting the Dedication of the Temple have been excavated. The *shammash* for this *hanukkiah* must have been a separate lamp.

The lamp in Figure 6 is a contemporary interpretation of this ancient form. It is very simple to construct. The drawings (Figure 7) show the approximate shapes to be cut from a ½-inch-thick slab of clay (the main piece is an oval folded around a wad of newspaper). Since the vessel will contain oil, it is very important for it not to leak. Make sure to seal all of the joints adequately, using vinegar in the clay slip mixture and sufficient pressure. Since an unglazed pottery lamp will absorb the oil, it is advisable to glaze your lamp. *Halakhic* requirements in fact specify that unless a ceramic Hanukkah lamp is glazed, it is to be discarded after use because it can't be made ritually clean again. If you are firing

*Reproduced in the *Encyclopaedia Judaica*, vol. 7, p. 1294.

6 Ceramic oil lamp.

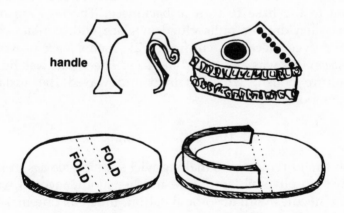

handle

FOLD FOLD FOLD

7 Diagram of the oil lamp's parts.

to stoneware temperatures, however, you can do without the glaze, since the clay body becomes vitreous. Even though the lamps shown here and in Figure 3 are stoneware fired at very high temperatures, making the clay no longer porous, the glaze makes cleaning easier and also enhances the surface.

Like many antique oil *hanukkiot*, the lamp shown in Figure 8 employs small glass vials as oil containers. Unlike their predecessors, however, these containers were not especially crafted with Hanukkah lights in mind; they were manufactured as replacement tops for coffee percolators and were transformed into oil receptacles by removing their metal collars and turning them upside down. Coffee-pot replacement tops are sold in a number of different sizes and shapes in most hardware shops and five-and-ten-cent stores. A frame to hold them is all that is necessary to convert them into a Hanukkah lamp. A hanging lamp could be made by wiring the glass jars to a sheet-metal backpiece. Since the earliest oil lamps are thought to have been collections of individual containers placed on a low pedestal base, I decided basically to follow that example.

The bench pedestal was made from a pine board 5½ by 20 inches, which was cut in half lengthwise with an undulating line: Nine scallops were drawn on the board freehand and then cut with an electric scroll saw (a coping saw could have been used). The scallops define the spaces where the glass jars sit. The other half of the board was glued and nailed to the base to form a backpiece. The legs are mushroom-shaped wooden drawer pulls glued in place with contact cement. An additional curved piece was cut from a 2½-inch square of wood to raise the *shammash*; this was also glued in place. The wood was finished with dark furniture polish, which stained and waxed the surface in one simple operation.

Wicks for Oil Lamps

A Turkish friend remembers making wicks, called *mechas* in Ladino, for her family's tin olive-oil lamp. She and her mother would wrap 2½- to 3-inch pine needles with absorbent cotton, much as one makes a cotton swab (the whole needle, however, not just the tip, was wrapped with

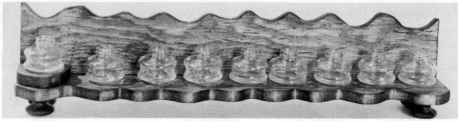

8   Glass and wood oil-burning *hanukkiah*.

the cotton). The lamp they used had rather deep containers for the oil, so the entire length of the pine needle was needed to absorb the oil, leaving about ½ inch above the oil line which continued to burn. There were no special games or other festivities associated with Hanukkah during my friend's childhood in Turkey; Purim was celebrated more amply. Making the wicks with her mother was both pleasant and memorable and provided that aura of anticipation one associates with a forthcoming holiday.

Ordinary pipe cleaners (use half for each wick) work very well in a similar way and remain in an upright position if the wire is formed into a small circle at the base. Cotton package-wrapping cord can also be used for wicking. Some kinds of twine work better than others, so you will have to experiment. In any case, twine has a tendency to lean, so I prefer the pipe cleaners.

Another type of early lamp was a circular one, often shaped like an eight-pointed star. These too are believed to be descendants of Graeco-Roman types. Care was taken to keep the receptacles for oil far enough apart, so that even though the lamp was circular, it would not resemble an open fire. These lamps were in use until recent times. They were carved from stone among the Jews of Yemen. Metal star-shaped lamps that were suspended from the ceiling were used in Spain and Italy and were very common in Germany.

Here is a not-quite-circular lamp that can be very simply made in an afternoon.

Glass beads from Hebron, which are available in hobby shops, were used to ornament the sand-cast plaster lamp shown in Figure 9. This lamp takes some planning and preparation, but it is very simple and fast to make. It is a lot of fun to do with children, who love to dig in the sand. Ordinary river, beach, or sandbox sand will do. Depending on where you live, sand can be bought at lumberyards, hardware stores, garden and landscape supply houses. I know people who have done sand casting right on the beach, but it is usually a bit chilly at Hanukkah time. A large bucket will hold about twenty-five pounds of dry sand. Dampen the sand with enough water to give it maximum binding consistency. Pinch it and see if it holds its shape. When it does, transfer the damp sand to a container that is about the same depth as you want your lamp to be. (When working with children, they can make small castings to accommodate birthday candles or Israeli Hanukkah candles.)

9 Sand-cast plaster lamp.

The container can be a cardboard box or a plastic basin. The lamp shown here was made by digging three large depressions in the sand with a trowel. The trowel was also used to texture the interior walls of these depressions. When filled with plaster, the depressions form the legs of the lamp, and the flat top surface holds the candles. Anything will balance on three points; if you try to make four legs, you might still end up having only three of them resting on the table. After the three depressions were dug, the glass beads were pressed into the sand so that half of each one would be imbedded in the plaster and the other half would show on the outside through the sand.

If you plan to make a large casting, it is a good idea to reinforce the plaster with wire screen or pieces of wire cut from a metal hanger. Cut the pieces of screen or metal beforehand because the plaster sets very quickly, and you will not have time once the plaster is mixed.

Plaster of Paris can be bought in any hardware or paint store and usually has directions right on the package. The plaster should be the consistency of thick cream. If it is too thin, it will obliterate any textures or designs you have made in the sand. If it is too thick, the detail might be lost. Add the plaster powder very gently and gradually to the water by the tablespoonful. Use a container you plan to throw away, like a two-pound coffee can. The action doesn't begin until the mixture is stirred, so do not agitate the water until all of the plaster has been added. Keep adding plaster until dry patches begin to form on the surface. Then it is time to stir. Use your hand to squeeze all the lumps out. Gently drip the plaster through your fingers into your sand carving, being careful not to disturb the design. When one layer of plaster has been poured, place the wire-screen reinforcement pieces in place, then continue adding plaster until the sand mold is filled. As the surface begins to firm up, use a candle of the same size as those you are ultimately planning to use to press nine depressions into the top of the lamp. (Do *not* pour any unused plaster down your drain. Let it harden in the mixing container, then discard container and plaster together.) Allow the plaster to set for at least half a day before removing it from the sand. Rinse the excess sand away with a fine spray of water.

Many variations are possible with this technique. Nine holes can be dug in the sand, and when the casting is removed, these stalagmite forms can serve as the candle-holders; the lamp stands on the flat surface that was on top when the plaster was poured. For a striated effect, different-colored sands can be layered before the digging is begun.

The frequent upheavals in Jewish life have made it impossible for historians to definitively trace a consistent chain of development of the form and decoration of the Hanukkah lamp. There are long periods of time and many places of settlement about which little or nothing is known. By the Middle Ages two types of metal *hanukkiot* had become common: the bench form, with an attached back piece, and the menorah form.

The bench form probably developed over the course of time by attaching the small individual oil lamps to one another in a row. When the lamps moved from the street into the house and it became customary to hang them, the back was necessary as a hanging device and a safety precaution. It also provided a place to attach the *shammash* slightly apart from the holy lights.

The backpiece, which is believed to have originated in Spain, provides an ideal surface for embellishment. The variety of styles and motifs used in different countries over the centuries to decorate this basically simple form is staggering. Architectural shapes are commonly used to represent the Temple, but the style of the architecture will usually be that of the country and period of the lamp in question. Therefore we find lamps that resemble Gothic or Russian Orthodox churches, Islamic mosques, and Italian palazzi. Hebrew quotations are often used as a decorative device as well as for the message they impart. Three of the phrases that appear with frequency, any of which would be suitable for your own Hanukkah craft projects, are:

"These lights are holy."	הנרות הללו קדש הם
"For the commandment is a lamp and the teaching is light." (Proverbs 6:23)	כי נר מצוה ותורה אור
"Blessed are you at your coming and blessed are you at your leaving." (Deut. 28:6)	ברוך אתה בבאך וברוך אתה בצאתך

The last quotation is reminiscent of the period when the *hanukkiah* was hung at the entrance to the house.

Flora and fauna of every description, both real and imaginary, have been used to ornament the *hanukkiah*. The serpent, an ancient Jewish symbol that is used frequently in Islamic art, found its way to the back piece of many lamps made in Moorish Spain and then later to those countries where the Sephardim settled after their expulsion by Ferdinand and Isabella. The hanging lamp shown in Figure 4 is from Spanish Morocco. It could have been made anytime between the sixteenth and nineteenth centuries, since the same molds were in use for three hundred years. The two other *hanukkiot* in Figure 4 are ornamented with symbols more typically identified as Jewish. Both of these brass oil lamps are from Poland. The taller of the two was probably made about the beginning of the eighteenth century. Each bird on the back piece has a hook, one to hold the *shammash* and the other a small brass pitcher symbolic of the miraculous cruse of oil. Since the ring at the top of the lamp enables it to be hung, the side panels may very well be later additions that permit it to be placed in a window or on a table. The side panels also serve as holders for Sabbath candles. This form of double-purpose lamp emerged in Poland during the eighteenth century and became popular throughout Eastern Europe.

Although oil continues to be used today for *hanukkiot*, candles have been widely used since before the end of the nineteenth century, when the other Polish lamp in Figure 4 was made. The legs are an integral part of the bench holding the candlesticks, since this lamp was never meant to be hung. Whereas the older lamp shows Spanish influence in its design, this one bears a strong resemblance to lamps made in Germany. The back is decorated with symbols that span centuries of Jewish iconography, incorporating in one design a seven-branched menorah, the most ancient of Jewish symbols, crowned and guarded by rampant lions, and a *magen David*, the newest and now most common Jewish symbol.

The human forms that have been used to decorate Hanukkah lamps include many familiar biblical figures, often honoring the original owner of the lamp whose name was that of the particular figure depicted. Not

10 The Yiddish inscription on the wooden panel behind this lamp, made of small lead chairs set into a wooden bench, says, "This Hanukkah lamp was made for his Bar Mitzvah in 1872 by the martyr Chaim Ari Zeifert, cantor and *mohel*. He was born in Mischelenitz, greater Krakow, in 1859 and killed by the Nazis in Auschwitz in 1942." The lamp was donated to the YIVO Institute for Jewish Research by his grandson in 1951 and is reproduced here with the permission of YIVO.

surprisingly, Judah the Maccabee and Judith, holding the severed head of Holofernes, adorn many lamps. Although it is historically unprovable that a beautiful widow named Judith saved the town of Bethulia from destruction by beheading the enemy general, the message of the apocryphal Book of Judith—that ingenuity and bravery can triumph over power and brutality—has firmly kept the story alive in Jewish folklore, wherein Judith is identified as a member of the Hasmonean family. Figures from non-Jewish mythology, such as Caritas, representing charity, and galloping centaurs, have also sometimes found places on Hanukkah lamps. Lamps from the Moslem world have often been decorated with the "hand of Fatima" to ward off malevolent spirits.

Another unexpected but not uncommon decorative device employed on Hanukkah lamps has been the use of coats of arms and national emblems. Among the most curious of these is a series of elaborately worked bronze sixteenth-century lamps ornamented with the armorial bearings of Roman Catholic cardinals. Both the Russian eagle and the two-headed German eagle have been depicted on *hanukkiot*, as has the portrait of Kaiser Joseph II of Austria. While these more pretentious lamps were usually made in the larger cities, lamps such as the one shown in Figure 10 were made of humble materials by folk artists in rural villages. Unfortunately, not many of these survive.

Until the twelfth century, when it became customary to kindle the lights in the synagogue for the benefit of travelers and the destitute who often spent the night there, the Hanukkah lights were kindled only at home. The bench-type lamp, which is ample and convenient for domestic use, seems small when used in a large public environment, so it was not adapted for synagogue use. Perhaps it was also reasoned that adding two branches to the menorah changed it sufficiently; thus the proscription against duplicating the Temple candelabrum wasn't violated. By the fifteenth century large menorah-form *hanukkiot* were commonly used in synagogues throughout Europe. Soon smaller ones were being made for domestic use. The menorah-form lamp, like the bench-type *hanukkiah*, has been made in a great variety of materials and styles.

The ceramic lamp in Figure 11 was made as an interpretation of the menorahs frequently shown on Polish paper cuts. It is, in fact, similar to the paper cut used as a party invitation on page 55. It was made by cutting a one-inch-thick slab of clay, which had been very well kneaded to get the air bubbles out, into the desired shape. The base was formed

11 Brown menorah-form ceramic lamp.

separately, and when both were leather hard, the two were carefully joined, using thick liquid clay moistened with vinegar. It was necessary to fill the base with newspaper in order to support the weight of the clay slab. The lamp was kept covered by towels and/or plastic to insure very slow drying and avoid cracks. The newspaper burns away in the kiln. The insides of the candle cups are glazed.

Today lamps continue to be made in the traditional bench and menorah forms, but they are also made in a wide variety of contemporary and individualistic styles, depending on the skill and materials available. In this century, as in previous ones, *hanukkiot* have been made from precious materials as well as from whatever was at hand under conditions of adversity. We know that scraps of wood and wire were made into lamps in the concentration camps during World War II. The Jewish Museum has in its collection a lamp made during the Korean War by an American soldier from parts of brass shell casings. Travellers in Israel during Hanukkah of 1973 often described an area in the Golan Heights, where some of the fiercest battles of the Yom Kippur War took place. Here huge *hanukkiot* were made out of shell casings embedded in stones and cement to stand as monuments to the fallen. They were lit each night of Hanukkah.

The lamp shown in Figure 12 is less dramatic than those just described, but it is a blessing to live in a peaceful place where a *hanukkiah* from an egg carton is more appropriate than one from a shell casing. Egg cartons are incredibly versatile, and when impregnated with white glue or wallpaper paste, they become very strong and durable. Since they are abundantly available, cut several apart into their component units and play with them as though they were children's building blocks until you have an arrangement that satisfies you. Then, using masking tape, join the parts together; reinforce all the seams with

12 Papier-mâché lamp made from an egg carton.

more masking tape. I used three lengths of ½-inch-wide copper tubing from a plumbing-supply store to make three legs, which I threaded through holes cut in the egg-carton cups. The tops of the legs serve as candle-holders. Six additional ½-inch lengths of tubing were then glued in place with liquid solder to form the remaining candleholders. When the basic structure is complete, coat the carton with a mixture of wallpaper paste and white glue and several layers of newspaper and/or paper towel dipped in the paste mixture. The more papier-mâché you use, the stronger the lamp will be. If it is getting too soggy to handle, let it dry overnight. (The oven, with a pilot light but no other flame, is fine for drying papier-mâché.) When enough papier-mâché has been applied to cover and strengthen the structural seams and joints, dry the lamp thoroughly. Then the lamp can be painted any way that pleases you. Before painting, I coated it with acrylic modeling paste, which provides a pleasant textured surface. Acrylics were then used to finish the painting.

We have had a glimpse at how rich and varied the ornamentation of the Hanukkah lamp has been. In lamps from all over the world there are abundant examples of *hanukkiot* that incorporate popular local motifs into the traditional form of the lamp, uniting the craftsman with his country and period. The lamps in Figures 13 and 14 were made to this end (slightly tongue-in-cheek), using as they do a national symbol in the first lamp and a commercial by-product in the second.

I never went to Sunday school as a child. Instead I attended one of the many *Yiddishe shules* that then flourished in the Bronx. These cultural schools, some of which continue to this day, were largely secular in their point of view, emphasizing Jewish survival through *Yiddishkeit*. Just as the Sunday schools do now, the *shule* would have children's performances to celebrate the various holidays. One I remember vividly took place on Hanukkah the year I was eight or nine. Eight of us, draped in sheets, wearing paper crowns, holding books in our left hands and candles in our right, were lined up across the stage. A ninth child (the *shammash*) lit our candles one at a time. As she did so we raised our candles in the air and recited a line from Emma Lazarus' poem "The New Colossus": "Give me your tired, your poor,/Your huddled masses yearning to breathe free,/The wretched refuse of your

13 Statue of Liberty lamp.

teeming shore."* The parents wept, and we were proud. Because that poem was us. Our parents had immigrated to the Land of the Free, the *Goldene Medina. We* were the wretched refuse and we were breathing free. It was a great feeling.

The Hanukkah lamp shown in Figure 13 was made not only to recapture childhood feelings but also to show that just as Jews have become an integral part of the American scene, so can a classical American symbol be used to express a Jewish theme. Some people may object to my use of "Liberty Enlightening the World" (the official title of the monument) in this way; others might say that I was desecrating the concept of a Hanukkah lamp. Humor, however, is very much a part of the human experience, and we Jews are known for our sometimes sardonic humorous expression. Too often painful jokes have best expressed the mood of the time. Perhaps this is a moment in history when as Jews in a democratic America our laughter can be whimsical

*The sonnet was written in 1883, four years before the poet's death at the age of thirty-eight. It was sold at auction for fifteen hundred dollars to raise money to build the pedestal for the Statue of Liberty. In 1903, at the crest of the last great wave of European immigration, the final five lines were engraved on a plaque and attached to the pedestal. It was a fitting memorial to this talented woman, a friend of Emerson and Longfellow, who had done volunteer work with refugees and vigorously spoken out in support of the "foreigners" who were so often attacked.

and joyful. Surely there are, and probably will continue to be, enough experiences that give rise to the more familiar bitter varieties of humor.

The lamp was constructed in two sessions, using "Made in Hong Kong" Statues of Liberty I had purchased from souvenir shops in the Times Square area of New York City. The statues come in so many sizes and materials that no single shop had enough of one kind to make up the total I needed. I never did find a matching ninth for the *shammash*, so I made it out of a large scrap of wood, which enabled me to have more space for writing the full text of the poem.

The base was constructed by gluing a 23-inch piece of stock 1½ x 2" wood to the center of a 24-inch piece of 2 x 4". Contact cement was used for this because of its great strength. This pedestal was coated with white glue, and the five-and-ten-cent-store American flags were gently laid in place. The sewn edging was cut away before gluing the flags in place so that the flags would lie flat and there would be no ridges between them. The *shammash* backpiece was similarly covered with a pair of larger flags. In all, eight flags were used, seven small (6 by 8 inches) and two larger (9 by 11 inches). An additional coat of white glue (which dries clear) was brushed over the surface of the applied flags to seal the cloth and wood.

While the pedestal was drying, I cut off the points from the bottom of birthday candleholders and glued them to the torches of the statues, which I had gently filed in order to roughen the surface and insure adhesion. For this I used a fast-drying multipurpose glue, which was then also used to glue the statues to the pedestal.

A word must now be said about the positioning of the statues. I initially decided to have Ms. Liberty alternately facing front, back, and to the sides in order to provide visual variety and to avoid giving a "backside" to the *hanukkiah*. Since the lettering goes all the way around the pedestal and the *shammash* base, the lamp can be viewed from any side and used as a decorative table centerpiece.

As I was placing the statues, it occurred to me that the piece was also a bit of historical commentary. The Statue of Liberty, a gift from France to America in 1886, has stood at the entrance to New York Harbor as a beacon of hope to millions of immigrants seeking a new life. But there have been times when Ms. Liberty has looked away and America has closed its doors to the persecuted and the downtrodden, as when the steamship *St. Louis* was denied haven in Miami and nine hundred Jews were sent back to Nazi Germany. So this can be construed as a gentle chiding of our sometimes unfortunate immigration policies.

The lettering was done the following day, after all the glue had dried. Several sizes of letter stencils were used. Using a *waterproof* felt-tip marker, I drew in the stencil letters, sometimes filling them in and sometimes leaving them hollow, as it pleased me. Beginning on the *shammash* back piece and ending on the statue pedestal, the last six lines of "The New Colossus" were used. The lettering took longer than any other procedure. After completing it, I used a fast-drying spray varnish over all. This caused the lettering to "bleed" slightly, further bonding it to the fabric.

The New Colossus

Not like the brazen giant of Greek fame,
With conquering limbs astride from land to land;
Here at our sea-washed, sunset gates shall stand
A mighty woman with a torch, whose flame
Is the imprisoned lightning, and her name
Mother of Exiles. From her beacon-hand
Glows world-wide welcome; her mild eyes command
The air-bridged harbor that twin cities frame.
"Keep, ancient lands, your storied pomp!" cries she
With silent lips. "Give me your tired, your poor,
Your huddled masses yearning to breathe free,
The wretched refuse of your teeming shore.
Send these, the homeless, tempest-tost to me,
I lift my lamp beside the golden door!"

While we are in this whimsical frame of mind and in order to end this chapter on a "light" note with a lamp that can be made very simply and inexpensively in less than an hour, I would like to encourage you to try your hand at making a soft-drink-can *hanukkiah*. Any soft-drink or beer can is usable. Larger lamps could be made from coffee or shortening cans. While one can simply use the ordinary metal cans and then paint them if desired, I very much enjoy the idea of incorporating the product design of the can into the design of the lamp. As I was making my lamp from a 7up can, I had fantasies of a twenty-second-century archaeologist uncovering the lamp and coming to very erudite conclusions about the meaning of a nine-candle lamp that says, "7up."

14 *Hanukkiah* with a pun.

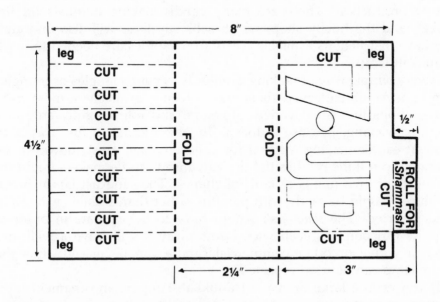

15 Diagram for soft-drink-can lamp.

Perhaps he will conclude that this slogan was the twentieth-century version of the seven-branched menorah we so often see on the back panels of traditional *hanukkiot* (see the Polish lamp with lions and menorah in Figure 4).

You will need a strong pair of scissors or metal shears and a needle-nose pliers. With the shears, cut away the top and bottom of the can, including the overlapping seam if there is one. Cut the resulting cylinder open so that you have a flat piece of metal roughly 4½ by 8 inches. Use a felt-tip pen or grease pencil to draw the cutting lines, as shown in Figure 15. Fold the metal as indicated in the drawing. Using your needle-nose pliers, curl the eight central strips of metal in a clockwise direction and press them sideways to the bench part of the lamp. Use the photograph and your imagination as a guide to form the legs and *shammash*. The lamp will accommodate standard-size Hanukkah candles.

Candles

For those people interested in the craft of candle-making, Hanukkah presents an ideal opportunity both for experimental work and for routine production. There are many candle-making manuals on the market, and the hobby shop, which sells supplies, will also undoubtedly have instructions available. Forty-four candles are needed for each Hanukkah lamp.

A very simple way of making candles is to cut rectangles or triangles from honeycomb-patterned sheet wax, which is available at most craft-supply shops in a great variety of colors, and roll it tightly around a length of wicking. Because it doesn't involve the use of fire, this is an excellent candle-making method for children; they must, however, be reminded to roll the candles tightly. Advanced candle-makers might try making their own molds in fanciful shapes. The sandcast lamp shown in Figure 9 could be made with paraffin rather than plaster, with eight wicks inserted. The *shammash* would have to be separate in order to fulfill its function. As each wick burns away it will leave a well into which a votive or other commercial candle can be placed; thus the candle lamp can be used repeatedly.

If you need a large dramatic Hanukkah lamp as an ornament for a meeting or party, you might consider using a large hunk of wood (either something lovely and wild from the woods or even a length of

2 x 4" lumber) and hammering nine nails into it from the underside, so that they form protruding spikes that can be driven into the base of large homemade candles. The candles can then be made by using frozen-juice containers or paper cups for molds. Making forty-four such candles to last for the entire holiday strikes me as rather boring for an individual, but it might be fun for a class. Earlier we discussed the awe in which light and fire are universally held. Perhaps now is the time to mention that part of that awe is due to fear—justifiable fear. If you are going to make candles, especially with children, do be careful, and follow safety precautions scrupulously.

Candle Boxes

Because I enjoy buying the colorful Israeli-made Hanukkah candles that are available very inexpensively in many supermarkets as well as in Jewish bookstores, most of my lamps were made to accommodate these. Others, such as the two menorah-shaped ceramic lamps (Figures 3 and 11), use standard household candles.

Whether or not you make your own candles, you might consider making a special box designed to hold forty-four candles of whatever size you need. Such a box with an appropriate design and inscription would also make a lovely and lasting gift. Boxes made of papier-mâché or painted and decorated cigar boxes make good projects for children. In the early years of American history the colonists were almost totally dependent on their own industry for everything they used. They laboriously dipped their own candles and then stored them in candle boxes. Often these, as well as boxes for salt and other necessities, were simply but beautifully decorated. Now, of course, they are highly sought after by collectors. Jewish ceremonial art also provides some inspired examples of ornamented boxes made for Sukkot and Shabbat. For Sukkot elaborate containers are made to hold the *ethrog*. The spice boxes made to hold the spices for the Havdalah ceremony are even more fanciful. Many of these are boxes in name only, since they have been made in forms as diverse as fish, flowers, deer, and towers. In past centuries it was often customary for the lady of the house to keep the things she carried on her person during the weekdays (such as a ring of enormous house keys) in a special box for the duration of the Sabbath. Perhaps we can combine Judaica with Americana by trying our hands at making Jewish-American boxes for Hanukkah candles.

Festivities at Home

From the end of November until January 1, when the nation collapses in relief with bellyaches, hangovers, and unpaid bills, Americans all over the country gorge themselves at one holiday party after another. After cleaning away the last of the Halloween candy, the revelry begins modestly enough with Thanksgiving, one of the few holidays which has not yet been totally ruined by overcommercialization and in which Jews can participate equally and with a full heart.

In some localities, where there is a sensitivity to the non-Christian communities, these parties bear names such as Winter Carnival, Snow Festival, Midwinter Break, and even Decemberfest. More common, however—and perhaps more honest—are those that are called Christmas parties. As soon as the Thanksgiving turkey carcass has been picked clean (if not before), the Christmas decorations go up, the carol music begins to play, and offices and classrooms all over the United States begin to prepare for Christmas with parties.

I would imagine that all of us have, at one time or another, with more or less discomfort or enjoyment, participated in some form of Christmas party. Unless one becomes a hermit every December, it is all but inevitable. So it is not lack of parties that prompts me to write this chapter on Hanukkah parties but rather a desire to explore some ways for making a midwinter holiday party into an authentically Jewish celebration.

During the years my family lived in Catholic Spain, we did not face this problem. The Spaniards use an absolute minimum of decorations (in Madrid, for example, only one or two of the principal shopping streets have the ordinary trees strung with clear glass bulbs, which are almost invisible during the day and elegant at night). Green, red, and glitter do not take over everywhere (except in those places that have succumbed to Americanization). Christmas Eve is celebrated with quiet family dinners, and children are given gifts on January 6 (Twelfth Night, Three Kings Day, or Epiphany). Living in such an environment when my boys were young, it was possible to celebrate Hanukkah basically as I had as a child. This meant *latkes* several times during the week, Hanukkah *gelt*, dreidels, and a few small gifts. When the boys entered the American School of Madrid and then later the U.S. Air Force Base school, both they and my husband and I began to feel the pressures of the American Way of Christmas upon us. When we returned to the United States, we began the custom of having an annual Hanukkah *latke* party.

The most important thing about parties is the people. So we all have to agree on everyone we invite. This is not always easy! Everyone invites several people as his own "special" guests. Everyone is responsible for "hosting" those people in his age group. The parties are incredibly noisy, but so many people have told me that they rarely get invited to parties where they can bring their children that even with the prevailing aura of madness, I think it's worthwhile. Further, the feeling I want to have is that of a large extended family.

Sunday is the best day for this sort of party. (By the end of the day in midwinter most everyone is a bit restless, and it's nice to go out as a family.) Every Hanukkah will have at least one Sunday in it. If one is a strict Sabbath observer, it is impossible to prepare everything necessary on Saturday; and even if one isn't *Shomer Shabbat*, some guests might feel uneasy coming to a place where so much work had gone on on Shabbat.

As these parties grew larger each year, I found that it was impossible to invite people by telephone and began making and sending invitations. I make enough of these invitations to send to many friends who are out of town as well. We don't send Hanukkah cards as such. Usually we send cards at Rosh Hashanah; our friends can reply at the time of Christmas, Hanukkah, and New Year's. This makes it possible to keep in touch with people with whom we have only a once-a-year relationship.

Two invitations from previous years are shown in Figures 16 and 17.

16 Paper-cut *Hanukkiah*, used as a party invitation.

17 Paper-cut party invitation. This design was also developed with a seven-branched menorah and used as the basis of a crewel-embroidered *mizrah* in my book *The Work of Our Hands*.

They were both made as paper cuts, and then inexpensively printed by photo-offset onto colored card stock. In both cases the overall size is 8½ by 11 inches; the folded card was sealed with notary seals and sent through the mail without an envelope. The message was written on the base of the *hanukkiah* in the bird design and then folded down the center. In the case of the black *hanukkiah* I drew four colored flames with a felt-tip pen, because that year the party was on the fourth night of Hanukkah, and wrote the message below. The two side panels were folded toward the center and sealed with notary seals.

18   Silk-screened family photograph.

Silk-Screened Party Invitation

For the last year that my college-bound son would be living at home, I decided to be more ambitious and sentimental, and I used a family photograph as the basis for silk-screened party invitations. The hardest part of making such a photoscreen is getting the family to agree on a time to be photographed and to cooperate while a friendly photographer shoots picture after picture in the hopes of getting one good one. Once you have a photo you like, the rest is relatively easy.

Choose a photograph with good contrast between black and white. Decide on the rough size and proportions of your finished design, but before doing the actual layout, buy all the envelopes you will need. Nothing is as frustrating as having a pile of beautiful cards made and signed and nothing available to mail them in. If you want a very unusual size, you will either have to make your own envelopes or order them through a printing firm. Since both of these alternatives are time-consuming and expensive, I recommend buying standard-size envelopes (there are so many different possibilities) and designing the card to fit them.

The card shown here measures 9¾ by 11¾ inches and fits into a standard 10-by-12-inch manila envelope. It is easier to work on a large image, but it doesn't matter what size your photo is because the shop that prepares the photographic material for silk-screening can have it enlarged or reduced. Any photograph that has sharp blacks and whites can be made into a photoscreen. You may, however, want to personalize it further by doctoring the photo a little. Our original photo, for example, was a horizontal rectangle and had a heavily textured background (the dining-room curtains). Since I wanted the finished image to be a circle, I used a compass to draw a circle large enough to include all the necessary parts of the image. Then I trimmed away the background and glued the cut-up photo of the silhouetted family into position in the circle. Since the edge of the table did not fill out the bottom of the circle, I drew that in and blacked out the rest of the bottom curve. Using white India ink, I then very carefully added a few lines to define my hand, my husband's hand, and my son's shirt and hair. I wouldn't recommend touching up the faces because the slightest change can distort the total facial contour. If you want a message to be part of your design, add it to the layout. This can be handwritten, with or without a stencil. You can also buy letters of all sizes and styles which have an adhesive on the back and can be applied in any design you like. I didn't put a message on my layout, preferring to handwrite individual messages and notes to accompany each one. As you can see in Figure 18, I signed and numbered each print, using the system of notation common to limited edition graphics. The fraction "1/60" means that the total number of prints in the edition was sixty and the example shown was the first one signed. Just as with any hand-printed graphic, there is slight variation between prints; the numbering, however, does not indicate a difference in quality. For some artists the numbers indicate the order in which the prints were done, but usually prints aren't numbered until they are completely dry, so many artists number them as they are sold. The numbering is just a bookkeeping device; the lower numbers do not signify a preferred print or higher value.

Basically, a silk-screened graphic is an image printed by a stencil method. With a photoscreen, such as the one I used, the photographic image is developed onto a light-sensitized screen. The white areas are those where the photographic emulsion was exposed to the light, and they now serve as a stencil, keeping the ink from passing through the silk. The photographic process can all be done at home, but even for the experienced artist it is a tricky procedure. There are many commercial firms that can use your photograph to make a screen, and you can still have the fun of printing it; check the Yellow Pages for photography shops that do this work.

Getting the photograph onto a silk screen is a two-step process. To get the same stark black-and-white effect you see in Figure 18 you will have to have a positive transparency made that will drop out all of the halftones from the image. This is called a *line* transparency (this means that anything that is more than 50 percent gray will print as black; anything less than 50 percent gray will print as white). Ask for a "line positive transparency on film suitable for developing onto a silk screen." If you are lucky, the same place that makes silk screens will be able to do all the photographic work for you too. The only way to find out is through persistent use of the telephone and specific questions. It is when the transparent positive is being made that the image is either reduced or enlarged in size. Then take the positive to a firm that specializes in silk-screen printing (phonebook, again) and have them develop the positive onto a screen of the size you need for your print. The squeegee (a rubber blade set in a wooden handle, which is used to push the ink through the screen) and ink can probably also be bought here.

For those of you who have never silk-screened before, I recommend looking at a book or two in the children's how-to section of your library. The process is simple, fun, and fast. More advanced printmakers who might want to do their own photographic work and perhaps even get into multiple-color work should, of course, consult serious printmaking books, such as *The Complete Printmaker*, by John Ross and Clare Romano (New York, The Free Press, 1972).

The silk-screen printing process is basically a method of making prints by forcing liquid colors through a screen that has a design stenciled on it. A wooden frame for the screen can be easily made at home, using 2 × 2" pine strips. The silk (nylon is often used) is then stapled around the edges of the frame. Very rudimentary silk-screen frames can be made by stretching a piece of silk or nylon in an embroidery hoop and using a piece of cardboard as a squeegee. Another simple silk screen can be made by cutting a window into the top of a shoe box and stapling a piece of silk over the opening. Commercial screens are readily available at hobby or art-supply shops.

The stencil design can be applied to the silk in a variety of different ways, including painting directly onto the silk with water-soluble glue or cutting stencils from special silk-screen film or from ordinary paper. In the case of the print shown in Figure 18, the stencil was put on the screen photographically. Figure 19 shows all the supplies you will need to begin: the screen, attached to a baseboard with hinges, the squeegee, and ink. Later you will need solvent and paper towels for cleaning up.

The printing is very simple and goes quickly. First the paper, which has been trimmed to size, is positioned under the screen. A small quantity (several tablespoons) of silk-screen ink is placed on the screen along the top edge of the silk. Hold the squeegee with both hands and pull the ink across the screen toward you. This spreads the ink over the surface of the silk, squeezing it through the mesh onto the paper below in exactly those areas that are unprotected by the stencil. Rest the squeegee against the far inner edge of the frame and lift the screen to remove the print. Place your second sheet of paper in position and repeat the squeegee procedure.

It is a good idea to work with someone when doing silk-screen printing. That way someone will always have clean hands, and unsightly smudges on the paper can be avoided. In lieu of fancy drying

19 The studio at the end of the day. On the table are the cleaned screen and squeegee; prints and T-shirts hang to dry.

20 Invitation accompanying the silk-screened card.

racks, the prints can be hung back to back to dry on a clothesline. Prepare all of your paper before you begin. Once under way, the screen shouldn't be left to dry out while you search about for more paper the right size. The printing goes very quickly; my younger son, who was my "printer's devil" for this edition, and I were still steamed up and eager to keep going after finishing the sixty prints in the edition. He suggested making T-shirts for the family and went running back to the house while I kept screening onto anything I could find in my studio. I had to keep the screen moist to prevent the fine mesh from clogging with congealed ink. While he was gone, I silk-screened onto newspaper until some fabric left from a sewing project caught my eye, and I made several prints on that. One of these went to my mother as a *hallah* cover, and two others were turned into aprons for my daughter and myself to wear at the *latke* party, at which my husband and sons wore the matching silk-screened T-shirts.

Because I am hoping that many of these prints will be saved, perhaps as an example of Jewish-American customs in the 1970s, I did not write the party information on the card itself. Accompanying the card was the actual invitation, simply drawn on typing paper with a felt-tip pen and photocopied. I used a Hanukkah-lamp design that is a simple one-line doodle. The pen never leaves the paper. Start at the left-hand corner of the base and try it.

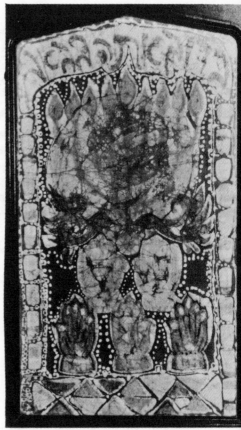

21 Ceramic bell.

22 Batik in door window.

DECORATIONS

Ceramic Bell

Once the invitations are out and I begin imagining my guests milling about the house, it becomes very important to me to provide a pleasant and aesthetic atmosphere for this once-a-year mixture of friends. I am the kind of housekeeper who leaves flowers around until they have gone to seed or turned into humus; any decoration I put up for a party is very likely to remain there until the next event comes along. Therefore, my inclination is either to use no decorations at all or to make things that are of a permanent nature and can be left up for a long time without getting tacky or irritating. With permanence (or at least reusability) as one of the considerations, I began making Hanukkah decorations. Later I will describe several simpler projects, but let me begin with objects that can be kept for years.

I had always wanted wind chimes on the front porch, so when I began thinking about Hanukkah decorations, I decided to make the chimes I had always wanted but to add a Hanukkah touch. The letters נ (nun), ג (gimel), ה (he), and ש (shin) are those found on the typical Hanukkah toy, the dreidel. When playing with the dreidel (see p. 117) the letters indicate the penalties of the game, but the letters have also been interpreted to stand for the phrase *nes gadol haya sham* ("a great miracle happened there"). As previously mentioned, it was once the custom to kindle the Hanukkah lights in the doorway, and they are still often put in the window to proclaim the miracle. Since the Maccabees rejoiced with music at the first Hanukkah, why not "proclaim the miracle" with the sound of wind chimes or bells? Bells are used in Christmas decorations, but unlike the tree or the wreath, which I will discuss below, bells remain a symbol common to both religions and one that I am not ready to relinquish. Bells are frequently used to ornament Torah crowns. The Liberty Bell in Philadelphia has inscribed on it a verse from Leviticus, "Ye shall proclaim liberty throughout the land unto all of the inhabitants thereof" (25:10). My bell is embossed with a pattern of eight-pointed stars. The eight-pointed star was one of the symbols on the coins minted during the Hasmonean dynasty. The clappers inside are either embossed or glazed with symbols from other Hasmonean coins or with letters.

The bell was made using the slab method of construction. This is a very direct approach to clay, not unlike carpentry or dressmaking. The clay was rolled out on a textured towel into a slab about 10 by 16 inches, and the designs—which had been made by carving them into pieces of hardened plaster of Paris—were stamped into the moist clay (see Figure 68). The embossed slab was then draped over an inverted flowerpot that had been padded with loosely wrapped newspaper. The "seam" was closed in the same manner that one seals a pie, using a thick mixture of vinegar and clay to help the edges adhere. Another thinner slab was rolled out, and the cookielike clappers were cut out and embossed. When the bell was dry to the leather-hard state, holes were made in the top to accommodate the copper wire that holds the clappers and the leather thong with which the bell is suspended from the porch ceiling.

If you do not have a kiln available but would still like to make a Hanukkah bell, consider making one from an inverted ceramic flowerpot, using clappers cut from pieces of tin cans. The whole bell could even be made from tin cans, but since they are less intrinsically handsome than terra-cotta flowerpots, you have to do some very special decorating to make them worth hanging. They do produce a pleasant tinkling sound.

Batik Door and Window Decoration

Today we think of doors in terms of security and of keeping people out. It is a refreshing change to remember that doors welcome our friends and set the tone for entry into our particular world. Because of their sheer size, doors are an inviting and challenging surface to decorate. But how does one decorate a door for Hanukkah? I began by looking into history, and my research unearthed a curious irony.

We have read in the First Book of Maccabees that when Judah and his men rededicated the Temple, they "decked the front of the Temple with crowns of gold and small shields." Crowns in that period were wreaths. We know that hellenization had been going on for well over a century, and in furniture and clothing styles the Jews had acquired a Hellenistic veneer. So it should not surprise us that when the Maccabees reclaimed the Temple, they ornamented it with golden victory wreaths. Another reason for the wreath is that originally Hanukkah was celebrated as a second Sukkot. In that period one of the manifestations of the holiday was that the participants wore leafy wreaths. There are depictions of wreaths on the synagogue ceiling tiles of Dura Europus, and they were carved into the second-century synagogue at Kfar Nahum (Capernaum). Indeed, the use of wreaths was so common in Jewish observance that in the fourth century C.E. a warning was issued to Christians by Ephraem the Syrian, an early church leader, to avoid the use of wreaths, since it "is the custom of Greeks and Jews." Obviously the Christians paid no attention to this injunction. Jews continued to use the crown as a symbol, but as fashions changed, the crown we commonly associate with Jewish decoration became a more modern, hatlike crown. Very early in the usage of the symbol of the victory crown the Jews reinterpreted it into a symbol signifying the majesty and dignity of the Law. In the synagogue the Torah scrolls are often embellished with elaborate and costly crowns. In the second century Rabbi Simeon ben Yohai said, "There are three crowns: the crown of learning, the crown of priesthood, and the crown of royalty; but the crown of a good name excells them all" (Pirke Abot IV, 17).

Although there are many symbols common to both Jews and Christians and although some (such as cherubim and bells) can be reclaimed without embarrassment, the wreath has become so totally identified with Christianity—and with Christmas in particular—that we are better off sticking to other versions of the crown motif. The vagaries of history are funny, and I cannot restrain a smile as I walk around town and see the evergreen and pinecone wreaths adorning the doors of my neighbors.

Having decided against making a Hanukkah wreath, I took a hard look at my front door and decided that what it really needed was a new curtain to replace the shabby piece of burlap that had been hanging there since we bought the house. I decided to do the curtain in batik, which would look like stained glass from the porch at night, when illuminated from the inside, and glow in the house with the morning light.

The batik shown in Figure 22 was designed to fill the peculiarly shaped window in my front door. Measure the window or door for which you are making the curtain, and leave enough extra material around the edge of your design to allow for the appropriate curtain

23 Paper-cut border design done for the Princeton Peace Center, based on pomegranate, star, and wreath motifs on the Kfar Nahum synagogue.

hardware. The design is a mixture of authentically Jewish motifs—the *hanukkiah* and the lettering—and those with a mixed pedigree. The inscription across the top reads ברוך אתה בבאך ("Blessed shalt thou be when thou comest in" [Deut. 28:6]). This expression is frequently found on old Hanukkah lamps and harks back to the days when it was the custom to hang the lamp in the doorway opposite the mezuzah. I wrote it in cursive Hebrew characters because they lent themselves to the curve of the window and because they always seem more intimate, in that script is more frequently used for ordinary handwritten messages. The *hanukkiah* is set against a large yellow sphere to give it greater luminosity. At either side of the lamp are two birds signifying—as they do for many peoples, including the Jews—peace and domesticity. At the bottom are five amuletlike hands, one for each member of my family. The hand amulet (or *hamsa*, as it is known from the Arabic word for "five"—the five fingers of the hand of God*) is a commonly used form of "protection" throughout the Middle East. Among Moslems it is known as the hand of Fatima. In other parts of the world the hand is also used as a charm against the "evil eye" but is depicted differently. In Brazil, for example, a three-dimensional fist with two fingers extended is common. The Jews have always had conflicting feelings about the use of amulets. Rabbinic and rationalistic Judaism, as we are familiar with it, is unequivocally opposed to the use of amulets. Nevertheless, since earliest days Jews have made and worn lucky charms of one sort or another. The hand has always been popular. It conveys the impression of both protection—in a "keep away" gesture—and blessing. Among Syrian Jews it was the custom, and perhaps still is in the sadly depleted remaining Syrian-Jewish community, to give the children Hanukkah gifts of candles in the form of a hand as protection against the "evil eye." In recent years, with the influx into Israel of Jews from non-European countries, the *hamsa* has become quite popular both as a wall decoration and in the form of

---

*The hand of God has appeared regularly over the centuries as a motif in Jewish art. It has been used in sacred book illustrations and set in mosaic on synagogue floors (Beth Alpha), and it appears in five of the paintings on the Dura Europas (Syria, third century) synagogue walls: the *Akedah* (binding of Isaac), the Exodus, Moses and the Burning Bush, Ezekiel's prophecy of the raising of the dry bones, and Elijah reviving a child. The strong saving hand of God is shown as the underlying force that is responsible for the miraculous event portrayed. Since Hanukkah too is a time to talk of miracles, the symbol is one that can be meaningfully incorporated into designs for the holiday.

pendants. The shape of the amulet hands in the batik is derived from a silver *hamsa* belonging to a friend; she knew of my fascination with hands of all sorts and kindly allowed me to use it as a model.

Batik is essentially a resist method of obtaining a design on fabric, paper, or even wood. Although we will only be discussing fabric batiking, the techniques are basically the same for surfaces other than cloth. The process involves impregnating the fabric with hot liquid wax in those areas that are meant to resist the dye. Traditionally, when several colors are used, wax is applied to all of the area that is to resist the first color; the cloth is immersed in the dye bath; and then the wax is removed by ironing or boiling the fabric. The same process is repeated for the second and subsequent colors, wax being applied to those areas that are to remain untouched by the new color.

The wax can be applied with a brush or by using the traditional Javanese batik tool called a *tjanting.* Many versions of these are sold in hobby shops, and with a little practice they are not difficult to use. The tool consists of a small metal scoop with a tiny tube projecting from it, attached to a wooden handle. Dip it into the melted wax, kept hot in a double boiler, and "paint" with the liquid wax as it runs out of the tube's opening. I use a small piece of cardboard to cover this opening as I move the tool from the wax pot to the desired position on the fabric. You might want to practice doodling with the liquid wax on a sheet of aluminum foil until you feel you can control the size and shape of the lines and dots you want to make. The cooled wax can then be peeled off the foil and returned to the wax pot.

Ordinary paraffin sold in supermarkets and hobby shops can be used for the wax. Although common household dye can be used for batik, I prefer using those dyes made especially for the process. They come in a better range of colors that remain intense even though the dye bath is cold (which it must be so as not to wash away the wax). Several brands of batik dye are available. Some come with a fixative powder right in the package; for others the fixer must be bought separately.

I wanted the batik to have many colors, but I was unwilling to go through the traditional batik process of multiple waxing and dyeing operations. The following batik method therefore is slightly unorthodox, but the results were pleasing, and it was spontaneous and relatively simple.

I drew a very light compositional sketch in pencil on the fabric; 100

percent cotton without a permanent-press finish will produce the best results. (Fabrics that are treated to resist soil also resist dye, and you will end up with pastel tints rather than strong colors.) I then mixed small amounts of batik dye in various colors with fixer and water and then painted in the areas and shapes I wanted. For this procedure the cloth was spread on a thick pad of newspaper.

When the design of birds, lamp, hands, lettering, and border triangles and squares had been painted and dried, I added some lines and details with *waterproof* felt-tip pens. I then applied the hot melted paraffin, using a brush for some areas and the *tjanting* for others. The type of brush that keeps the wax hot longest is a long-bristled nylon one. I applied the wax over all of the design I had previously painted, slightly enlarging each shape with an area of clear wax. This provides a lot of white space and adds to the luminosity of the design. It is important that the wax completely penetrate the cloth so that it will fully protect the areas you want to remain undyed by the background color.

Once the waxing was complete, I crumpled the fabric lightly to obtain the crackle lines that are characteristic of batik. This is an important step when using this method of spot-dye painting, because then the overall crackle effect unifies the background with the design. The entire curtain was then immersed in the cold-water dye bath, following the directions on the dye package, and all the wax was ironed out between sheets of newspaper. Using this method, my daughter and I made a number of other small batiks to hang in windows and to give away.

Mezuzahs

The Maccabees not only adorned the front of the Temple with crowns and shields, they also "dedicated afresh the gates." If you do not already have a mezuzah on your doorpost, Hanukkah is an ideal time to put one up. The one shown in Figure 25 is of dark-brown stoneware. White porcelain slip and glaze was used to accentuate the *magen David* and the carved *shin*. *Shin* stands for *Shaday*, one of the names of God, an acrostic of the three words שומר דלתות ישראל (Guardian of the doorways of Israel), and is written on the reverse side of every mezuzah scroll. If this is not visible through a small opening in the scroll container, then the word or its initial letter is put on the front of the container. The parchment scroll inside has inscribed on it two passages

24 Batiked fabric. The menorahs were done using the *tjanting;* the lions were made by dipping a lion-shaped cookie cutter into the melted wax and stamping it onto the fabric.

25 Ceramic mezuzah.

from Deuteronomy 6:4–9 and 11:13–21. The parchment scrolls should be checked twice every seven years to be certain that the writing has not faded. By the Maccabean period the practice of affixing a mezuzah to the doorpost was already ancient.

A Talmudic story is told about Rabbi Judah ha-Nasi and his exchange of gifts with the Parthian king. The king sent a magnificent pearl to Rabbi Judah, who responded by sending a mezuzah in return. The king was furious, feeling that he was being insulted. "The gift I sent was of inestimable value, and you have responded with a worthless trinket." Rabbi Judah explained: "Your gift is so valuable that it will have to be guarded, while the present I gave you will protect you even when you sleep." The "protection" afforded by placing mezuzahs on all the doorposts of a home is not that of a lucky charm, but rather of a belief that a dwelling place inscribed with a testimony of faith can be a sanctuary. It serves as a reminder to everyone as they enter and leave that this is a Jewish home committed to Jewish values.

Mizrahim

While it is true that the Jewish attitude toward decorations, whether of a permanent or temporary nature, has often been ambivalent, there is a uniquely Jewish form of adorning the eastern wall of a home. When the Temple still stood, Jews outside Jerusalem faced toward that city when praying. After the Roman destruction of the Temple in 70 C.E., with the subsequent dispersion of Jews all over the world, the practice of turning toward Jerusalem when praying continued. For many of the world's Jews, this meant facing east. The custom then developed of marking the eastern wall of the home in some manner so that one would always be aware of the direction of Jerusalem. Often this took the form of leaving a part of the wall unfinished or with exposed masonry, as though to say that as long as the Temple was in ruins so should this part of the house remain incomplete. In time, however, the practice developed of making an embellishment for that wall, always using the word *mizrah* מזרח (east) as the central part of the design. The ornament itself is also called a *mizrah*. *Mizrahim* have been made in many media, ranging from cut paper, which was very popular throughout Eastern Europe and North Africa in the nineteenth and early twentieth centuries, to painted and embroidered textiles, wood, ceramic, precious metals, and today plastics.

As well as the word מזרח, *mizrahim* will often have additional Hebrew phrases on them and be decorated with fanciful flora and fauna. Stylized reminders of the Temple, pillars, arches, shew-bread tables, and seven-branched menorot are other frequently used symbols.

Although I imagine they exist, I have only seen one *mizrah* made especially for holiday use. It is a lithograph printed in Israel for Sukkot. Aside from pillars festooned with leaves and flowers, it has a pair of cornucopias that drip roses and a central crowned medallion containing the word *mizrah*, with a rising sun glowing behind the letters. What makes this *mizrah* peculiar to Sukkot is that it also has the blessings that invite the seven patriarchs (*ushpizin*) to enter the Sukkah and participate in the holiday. There are elaborate little drawings emblematic of each of the *ushpizin*, enclosed in other medallion forms. Abraham is represented by a tent, Isaac by a ram caught in a bush, Jacob by a ladder, Moses by a Torah scroll and tablets of the Law, Aaron by priestly hands and breastplate, Joseph by sheaves of grain under a sky that is half stormy and half sunny, and David by a crown and fiddle. With its many colors and crude romanticism, the overall effect is bizarre but delightful.

Hanukkah is an ideal time to explore different ways of making a *mizrah*—either one suitable for year-round use, which could perhaps be given as a gift, or one designed specifically for the holiday. Three different possibilities are given on the following pages. When you do your own, you might want to combine ideas from one with those suggested by another, use materials found elsewhere in this book, or—even better—draw on your own life and experiences.

The first *mizrah* (Figure 26) is meant to be displayed all year, can be hung in any room of the house, and was made in less than an hour. A table jigsaw was used to cut the letters from lattice stripping, but a coping saw would also have done the job, albeit more slowly. The letters were then glued to a scrap piece of cedar shingle. The different wood tones contrast pleasantly in their natural state, but they could also have been stained or painted for a different effect. The hanger for the *mizrah* was made by attaching the ring from a flip-top soft-drink can to the back with a small nail.

The second *mizrah* was made for me by my grandfather's brother, the family patriarch, gently reminding us all of one another's existence. His ancestors were craftsmen, carpenters, and their skills were passed

26 Simple wood appliqué *mizrah*.

27 *Mizrah*. The central *magen David* says, "Zion"; the Yiddish border, "A Joyous Hanukkah to the Jewish People—Peace."

from generation to generation. He himself came to America from Poland in 1921 and continued his craft as a carpenter and staircase-builder. As he grew older, working with wood became increasingly difficult, so in recent years he has turned his abilities to making paper mosaic ornaments and greeting cards. Family occasions are commemorated by a special card from Uncle Leo, which is treasured and often framed. The letters are cut from a variety of patterned papers, including stamps, magazines, and old wallpaper samples.

The *mizrah* shown in Figures 28 and 29 was made with the intention of uniting some of the traditional imagery associated with the age-old yearning for Jerusalem with the present reality of Israel today. The form of a hinged triptych was used because it enables two images to be presented simultaneously, almost as a narrative. On the outside, when the panels are closed, there is a sketchy cityscape, the blue and white "clouds" floating overhead spelling out in crenellated lettering "Jerusalem." When opened, the image changes dramatically. The city is divided, the colors are now those of fire and violence (red, yellow, and black). Only the word *mizrah* is white, with purity and hope. The form is traditional: The two side panels are reminiscent of the Temple pillars, the arch shape of a window or perhaps of the Temple itself. In the center is a *hanukkiah* in menorah form. Upon close inspection you will notice that the lamp is made up of a collage of newspaper photos, some from World War II but most from Ma'alot. The lone ballerina is there by way of contrast and hope (a reference to the Panovs' recent immigration to Israel from Russia) and to visually lead one to the newspaper clippings. I've used the same photographs several times. The side panels read, "Not by might, nor by power," and below the lamp the words "But by my Spirit" are painted. It is indeed by the spirit of the martyrs and fighters that the lamp of dedication continues to be lit.

Hanukkah Needlepoint

The needlepoint wall hanging shown in Figure 30 was made for Hanukkah, but its message is so universal and timely that it can easily remain up all year. The phrase

לא בחיל ולא בכח כי אם־ברוחי אמר יי צבאות

("Not by might nor by power but by My Spirit Saith the Lord of Hosts"

28 Closed triptych *mizrah*.

[Zech. 4:6]) is the penultimate one of the prophetic biblical portion read
in the synagogue on the Sabbath of Hanukkah. This verse reflects the
religious emphasis placed on the Maccabean military victory.

The Hebrew quotation was worked in three shades of yellow on a
deep red background. Red represents warfare, and yellow, light; together they are the colors of flame. The English translation was worked
in an even darker shade of red. The intention was to have the viewer
read the English almost subliminally and at least to feel as though he
were reading Hebrew.

The drawing shown in Figure 31 can be enlarged photographically
or manually to any size you like. Simply draw a grid on your paper and
copy the drawing square by square. When the drawing is complete,
color in the letters so they are easily visible through the canvas, and

29 Open triptych *mizrah*.

place the canvas over the drawing on a large work surface. Make sure the canvas and drawing remain stationary (use tape, tacks, or heavy books around the edges) while you trace the drawing onto the canvas with waterproof felt-tip pens. Remember to leave at least two inches of canvas outside the design so you can stretch and mount the work properly when it is finished. Put masking tape around the raw edges of the canvas before you begin to work so the canvas doesn't unravel.

The finished work was blocked and mounted simultaneously. This was done by using artist's canvas stretchers. Canvas stretchers are available in art-supply stores and come in many lengths. Two 16-inch and two 24-inch stretchers were assembled into a rectangle in minutes. The needlepoint was dampened quite thoroughly on the reverse side*

---

*If your finished canvas shows only a minimum of misshaping, you can staple it onto the frame while it's still dry. Then hold a steam iron close to the work but not quite touching it so that the steam penetrates the needlework. Let the steamed canvas dry thoroughly. This short-cut method will block any wood needlepoint that hasn't been badly distorted during the working.

30 Needlepoint wall hanging.

and power-stapled to this wooden frame to dry. Don't be alarmed if the damp work stretches and sags; it will flatten out as it dries. Just make certain that you staple the four midpoints of the sides in place first. When the work is dry, you can have it framed or use inexpensive lattice stripping from the lumber yard to make a simple finishing edge.

If some of the decorations just described seem to require more ambition than you are in the mood for, consider adapting some of the motifs they contain and executing them by the following simpler techniques for children's projects in the next chapter.

31 Pattern for needlepoint.

THE "LATKE" PARTY

It is said that fried food for Hanukkah is popular because cooking with oil is reminiscent of the Hanukkah miracle. Depending upon where they have lived, people have adapted local recipes and originated a large number of pancakes, fritters, and fried pastries for Hanukkah. Since the largest percentage of American Jews are of Eastern European background, we tend to think of that relative latecomer to the Hanukkah menu, the potato *latke*, as the sole Hanukkah food.

During the Middle Ages favorite Hanukkah dishes were generally dairy foods, and many delicacies including *latkes*, were made with cheese. This custom is said to have stemmed from the story of Judith, who gave Holofernes cheese to eat, which made him thirsty. He quenched his thirst with wine, and she was able to behead him as he lay asleep in a drunken stupor. Since the story of Judith was thought to have been a source of inspiration to the Maccabees, cheese-filled pancakes, *kreplach* (dumplings similar to ravioli, filled with chopped meat or cheese), strudel, and other pastries are still often served during Hanukkah.

Unlike Passover, when many of the foods we eat or abstain from are indicated by the holiday ritual, the typical Hanukkah foods are seasonal or folkloric. Since Hanukkah is a winter holiday, traditional main courses around the world include hearty dishes such as South American *puchero* (meat and chick-pea stew), Greek *stifatho* (a beef casserole flavored with cinnamon and saffron), Dutch roast goose stuffed with apples, and various rice and lentil pilafs from India and the Middle East.

My Hanukkah fare is simple: Eastern European potato *latkes* and Israeli doughnuts. When the guests arrived for our *latke* party, they were not confronted with all the decorations described here or in the following chapter. The appliqué was made for the Jewish Center, the styrofoam prints were used to decorate a wall for an Israeli bond fund-raising dinner, and some of the other things were made for friends. The guests were welcomed by the bell, the batik in the door, the mezuzah, the needlepoint, and a *mizrah*. The papier-mâché elephant stood on a table along with two bowls, one full of assorted dreidels, the other with a mixture of raisins, nuts, and foil-covered coins to use as tokens in playing the dreidel game (see Figures 47 and 53).

We invite our guests to come in the late afternoon, so immediately after breakfast we all begin to grate potatoes and to chop and fry onions. By the time people begin to arrive, almost all of the *latkes* have been made. Our friends nibble on cheese and drink cider or sangria while they watch the last of the *latkes* being made. Those already made are kept warm in a huge roasting pan in a warm oven. By then I am ready to relax and spend some time with our guests, and there is always someone eager to take over the frying; this year seven friends took turns while onlookers kibitzed. The *latke* recipe is taped to the refrigerator while we are working and left up during the party, because I am invariably asked how many potatoes I used. I know that potatoes can be grated by an electric blender, but I persist in manual grating because I like the long stringy texture of the shreds. The recipe below has been reduced to family size.

Potato Latkes

9 medium-size potatoes	3 tablespoons flour
3 small onions, chopped	¼ teaspoon pepper
Salad oil	1½ teaspoons salt
3 eggs, slightly beaten	¾ teaspoon baking powder

Wash the potatoes thoroughly and remove any spots or blemishes. It isn't necessary to peel the potatoes. Grate them, using the coarsest side of the grater. Allow the grated potatoes to sit for 10 minutes, and then turn them into a colander, pressing out the accumulated liquid. Fry the chopped onions in enough salad oil to just cover the bottom of a skillet. Add the fried onions to the drained potatoes and stir in the eggs. Add the flour, pepper, salt, and baking powder and mix thoroughly. (More liquid will continue to form, but do not pour it off; occasionally stir the mixture as you remove spoonfuls for frying.) Drop the batter by tablespoonfuls into a large skillet containing about ¼ inch of hot salad oil. Flatten with a slotted metal pancake turner. When the edges of the *latkes* become brown, turn and brown the other sides. Drain on paper towels and then keep warm in a low (185°) oven until all the *latkes* are ready to serve.

The *latkes* are served with sour cream and homemade applesauce, which is made well in advance of our party in gallon batches. I use any apples I can get cheaply and adjust the sweetness with honey, brown sugar, and/or lemon juice.

By the time all the *latkes* have been made, even the latest of our guests has usually arrived and the sky is dark. With the food waiting in the oven, we all gather in the dining room, where four *hanukkiot* have been set out on the table. The overhead lights are turned off and the children, with help from the rest of us, say the blessings and light the candles.

The lamps are then placed on various windowsills and the dining-room table is laden with *latkes*, applesauce, sour cream, and the necessary plates and forks. Doughnuts—plain or jelly-filled—are served for dessert because *soofganiyot* are very popular in Israel at Hanukkah time.

OTHER HANUKKAH FOODS

The longer the Jewish community has stayed in a particular country, the more certain we are to find recipes of a hybrid nature. In communities that have existed for many centuries in their respective "host" countries, we often come upon traditional foods for the different Jewish holidays that combine the qualities and flavors of the local country with the religious, ceremonial, or folkloric requirements of the particular festival. Often Jewish festival foods will be not very unlike the special foods enjoyed by the local non-Jewish community on their holidays of the same season.

At Hanukkah and Purim in Turkey, for example, Jewish women make a sweet variation of the Turkish *bórek*, a cheese-filled turnover. The Jewish version uses thicker pastry dough cut into 2- or 3-inch rounds, which are filled with a mixture of ground walnuts, cinnamon, and sugar, folded over into small turnovers, baked, and then simmered in a very sweet sugar syrup not unlike that used for the Moroccan *fichuelas* on p. 83. The resultant pastry is soft, glazed, and unbelievably gooey-sweet.

Shaped cookies for holidays are popular throughout the world. A great variety of these are traditionally made for Purim, most typically the triangular *hamentash*, which is meant to look like the hat worn by the evil Hamen of the Purim story. Foods popular for one holiday often find their way to the festive board of another. The Turkish cheese pastries described above are an example of this, as are the cookies called *Sinterklaasjes*, which even Orthodox Jewish children in Holland find in the wooden shoes they set out on St. Nicholas Night, twenty days before Christmas. Today in Israel at Hanukkah time variations of this basic gingerbreadlike recipe are made in many shapes. There are some cookie cutters available for Hanukkah, but you might want to try making shaped cookies using some of the motifs suggested by this book and your own imagination. Any basic sugar-cookie dough can be used—half dark and half light, if you wish—and formed into Maccabees, Daniels, Judiths, elephants, lions, Hebrew letters, etcetera. Next Hanukkah I plan to get back to the Book of Daniel and make some of the strange beasts described in his visions. Children love to devour fantastic cookie creatures—and to make them.

Spanish Moroccan Dishes

The Jews were expelled from Spain in 1492, and many Spanish towns have no memory of their once-vibrant *Juderias,* the neighborhoods inhabited by Jews. In Madrid resettlement has been going on since 1869; nevertheless, the *comunidad Israelita de Madrid* is made up mainly of Jews who came to Spain after World War II. The new Spanish Jewish community had been raising money for years in the hopes of one day getting government permission to build a new synagogue in Madrid, the first in more than five hundred years. Finally they received permission, but when the Six Day War broke out, all the money was sent to help Israel. Afterward another fund-raising campaign was undertaken, and with the help of the Joint Distribution Committee, a new synagogue, Beth Yaacov, was consecrated in 1968. And so on a recent visit to Spain, I stopped to see the new synagogue and think of all the missing years in the history of Spanish Jewry.

Since my visit was made on a hot July afternoon, the synagogue was all but deserted. There was a uniformed policeman at the door, whose purpose I did not inquire into. A caretaker told me that the rabbi was on vacation and took me to the office of the receptionist, a man in his early forties. I told him that I was writing a book about Hanukkah and asked if there were any local customs of interest. He said that only the rabbi could *officially* tell me anything. So I gave up my professional line of inquiry, it being a hot and lazy afternoon, and we began to chat.

Soon the receptionist, a Moroccan Jew, was confirming for me what I had read in many places—that Hanukkah among Sephardic Jews is a very understated holiday and not at all like the American version. Purim, he insisted, is the time to give gifts to the children, have parties, play games, put on plays, make decorations, etcetera. He first became aware of the American Jewish custom, he said, when his family had taken in an American college student on her junior year abroad, and at Hanukkah the girl's family had sent presents to him and his family. He was very surprised at this, because Hanukkah observance for him means lighting the oil-burning *hanukkiah* the family brought with them from Morocco. He said that the Ashkenazic Jews in Madrid used candles, while the Sephardim favored oil lamps. But even among the Spanish Ashkenazim, Hanukkah remains a minor festival, and much more attention is paid to Purim.

As he warmed to the subject, he said, "You know, now that you mention it, on Rosh Hodesh we always have a special family meal, a little fiesta."

I hadn't been aware of mentioning Rosh Hodesh (the festival of the New Moon) at all. Seeing my puzzled look, he went on to remind me that since Hanukkah comes at the end of the month of Kislev, the sixth candle marks the beginning of the new month of Tevet. And on that evening the family gathers for a festive meal of *couscous*. This, he said, had been done in his family for as long as he could remember and was also customary among his friends. Yes, Rosh Hodesh Hanukkah was an especially important day. Since we were on the subject of food, I couldn't help but ask if, now that his memory was loosened up, he couldn't remember some other special goody from his childhood. And so he did.

"Talking about Hanukkah in July to an American does strange things to a man," he said, making a characteristic gesture of touching his forehead with his hand. "How could I have forgotten the *fichuelas*?" He then went on to tell me that throughout Hanukkah, but especially for Rosh Hodesh Hanukkah, his mother (and now his wife) made a delectable spiral-shaped fried pastry which was then dipped in a sugar glaze and eaten for dessert or at breakfast with coffee or at teatime. Plates of these were also given as gifts to friends and neighbors.

Getting the recipe from him was another matter. No matter how many times he had watched, he had never made them himself. We agreed that we'd have to find a woman experienced in the ways of *fichuelas* to help. He sent the caretaker, who had been listening silently to most of our conversation, in search of a Moroccan Jewish woman who could help us. In a little while the caretaker returned with a woman who, although more than willing to give us the recipe, insisted that without lifelong experience it couldn't be done outside of Spain or

Morocco. The difficulty, it seems, is in forming the spirals while they are being fried. Both she and the receptionist, as well as the silent caretaker, began gesturing elaborately. Nevertheless, I insisted that I would try the recipe back in my kitchen in Princeton. I have, and even though the technique of forming the spirals becomes easier the longer you practice it, it is by no means impossible for a beginner. Besides, as my Moroccan informant said, "Even if it doesn't look perfect, it tastes too good to throw away."

Fichuelas de Hanukkah

DOUGH:

5 cups flour
1 teaspoon salt
2 eggs, slightly beaten
¼ cup salad oil
¾ cup warm water

2 cups salad oil for frying

SUGAR GLAZE (*almibar*)

1¼ cups sugar
½ cup water

Measure the flour into a large mixing bowl and stir in the remaining dough ingredients in the order given. This will make a fairly stiff dough. Knead vigorously for five minutes on an *unfloured* surface or until the dough feels smooth and elastic. Divide the dough into 4 balls. Roll the first ball out on a lightly floured surface to make a rectangle about 9 × 18 inches. The dough should be as thin and translucent as possible. Cut the dough into 6 strips about 1½ inches wide and 18 inches long. (The dough will be easier to roll if it is tightly wrapped in plastic wrap and allowed to "rest" for at least an hour.)

Heat the 2 cups of salad oil in a small shallow saucepan. (Unlike *latkes*, you will only be making one *fichuela* at a time, so you will not need a large frying pan.)

Prepare the sugar glaze by heating the sugar in the water until it is melted but not brown. Keep warm while using.

Gently lift one end of a strip of dough in your left hand. Pierce the other end with a fork; place this end in the hot oil. As it fries, gently turn the fork, rolling the dough around it and forming a pinwheel. It goes very quickly, the dough puffing up to look like a pastry rose. Do not allow it to remain in oil long enough to brown. Even when fried, the dough should remain almost white, with a few golden spots. Use a slotted spoon to

32 The woman who gave me the recipe for *fichuelas* told me to use half an eggshell of oil for every egg—a more interesting if less exact measurement than the one I used.

remove the pastry from the hot oil and dip it immediately into the warm sugar glaze. Place on a plate to cool.

Repeat with all of the dough until you have 24 pastries. (Any scraps can, of course, be fried and glazed, but they won't be as elegant as the spiral.)

Basically, *couscous* is a cracked-wheat dish. The grain itself is used like rice or kasha and can be prepared and served with many different meats, vegetables, and sauces. Gourmet shops often sell a product not unlike semolina which is called *couscous* and which, like instant rice, is partially precooked. All that must be done is to allow the grain to steep in hot water for about half an hour. The recipe below can be made with this type of *couscous*, but I much prefer to begin with the coarsely milled wheat my friend at the Spanish synagogue recommended. It takes only five extra minutes, is less expensive, and tastes as well as looks better.

I have stayed as close to the original recipe as I possibly could with the *fichuelas*, but I decided to Americanize the *couscous* recipe even further by cooking the grain-and-meat mixture in a pumpkin rather than a casserole. Pumpkins are a lovely part of the American fall landscape. Perhaps using a pumpkin would be more appropriate for Sukkot than for Hanukkah, since the former is a harvest festival, but I'll justify its use by remembering that initially Hanukkah was identified as a second Sukkot. It is such a beautiful vegetable that it seems a pity to relegate it to pumpkin pie.

Couscous

One medium-size well-formed stemmed
   pumpkin, 10 to 12 inches across
1½ cups bulgur wheat (coarsely milled
   whole wheat, available in health-food
   stores)
3 cups boiling water
1½ teaspoons salt
3 tablespoons salad oil

1½ lbs. ground lamb
2 medium onions,
   coarsely chopped
2 stalks of celery, diced
3 tablespoons honey
¾ cup dark raisins
¾ cup dry red wine

Prepare the pumpkin by washing it and cutting a lid in the same way you would for a jack-o'-lantern. Remove the seeds and the fibers that hold them. Leave the pulp intact.

Toast the bulgur wheat in a large, lightly oiled frying pan over medium heat. Stir constantly for about five minutes until the color has darkened slightly and a nutlike fragrance is given off. Add the boiling water and the salt. Cover, and turn the flame as low as possible. Allow to steam for ½ hour or until all the water is absorbed.

Heat the salad oil in another pan. Add the ground lamb and chopped onions and brown. Add this to the wheat, along with the remaining ingredients (except for the pumpkin). Mix thoroughly.

Lightly oil the pumpkin skin (the oil will keep the skin from drying out and will help it turn a beautiful color). Stuff the pumpkin with the meat mixture and cover with the pumpkin lid. Place on a large cookie sheet and bake in a preheated 350° oven for 1½ hours. If all the lamb mixture will not fit into the pumpkin, bake the leftovers separately in a small covered casserole. (If you decide not to use the pumpkin at all, use a 3-quart covered casserole and bake the lamb mixture for 45 minutes. In that case,

33 *Couscous* in a pumpkin.

add a little water or wine if necessary to keep the mixture moist.)

You can tell when the pumpkin is cooked by lifting the lid and gently testing the pumpkin flesh with a skewer or fork. Don't pierce the skin or it will leak. When serving, scoop out some of the cooked pumpkin (which is a mildly flavored squash) along with the *couscous*. This will serve four to six hungry people.

Since the lamb mixture is mildly sweetened with the honey and raisins and the pumpkin is also slightly sweet, I like to use strong-flavored greens (such as raw spinach and watercress) along with raw mushrooms in the accompanying green salad. This could be followed by *fichuelas* and very strong coffee or tea for dessert. It makes a nice party menu for Rosh Hodesh Hanukkah.

PLATES FOR THE HANUKKAH TABLE

The plate used to serve the *couscous*-filled pumpkin, which is shown in full in Figure 34, is decorated with the Yiddish phrase *"A Yom Tov a Shayner"* ("a lovely holiday"). This is the second line of a Hanukkah song I enjoyed as a child.

Hanukkah, Oy Hanukkah	Hanukkah, oh Hanukkah,
A Yom Tov a shayner	A lovely holiday,
A lustiker, a fraylicher,	A lusty one, a joyous one,
Nito nokh azoyner!	There's none other like it!

This cheerful refrain has stuck with me over the years, and it gave me great pleasure to decorate the Moroccan *couscous* plate with a phrase from a Yiddish song. It pleases me too that the simple Hebrew script decoration is perfectly at home with the dinner plates from Spain, wine glasses I made when I was a student, and candlesticks from Eastern Europe. With this inscription, the plate can be used for any holiday.

Looking at collections of Judaica, one will find many examples of plates made for the Sabbath and for Passover. The contemporary American might be surprised to note that there are also quite a few special plates made for Purim. This is because one of the nicest Purim customs has been to exchange homemade pastries and cookies with friends and neighbors, and special plates were made to show off the delicacies. Very few plates or dishes have been made especially for

34 Wheel-thrown ceramic *"Yom Tov"* plate.

Hanukkah. To remedy this situation, I made the *"Yom Tov"* plate above as well as three others, all based on the same design, which was then used for a batik tablecloth. The design, which in its skeletal form appears in Figure 35, is composed of four interwoven *hanukkiot*. The sectioned dish in Figure 39 was made to accommodate the cheese and crackers served at both our *latke* party and a holiday cheese-and-wine party. One of the sections has a pattern of tiny menorahs carved into it.

The plates in Figures 36, 37, and 38 are all decorated with the same design of interlocking Hanukkah lamps. In each case a different technique was employed. Thus the dishes are related to one another but do not make a "set" in the usual sense.

The tablecloth in Figure 40 was made especially for our various Hanukkah parties, using the batik method. The same design of interlocking Hanukkah lamps was lightly drawn on the heavy cotton cloth and then waxed, using the *tjanting*. Since it is difficult to draw a

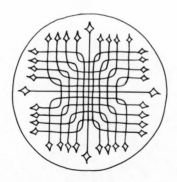

35 Interlocking Hanukkah lamp design. The design can be enlarged and used for anything from plates to cushions or, as I have done, for a tablecloth.

perfectly even line with the wax, I purposely paused at regular intervals, letting the line thicken, which gives the overall design an interesting character. The border design again employs lamplike forms as a motif, as well as pomegranates, an ancient fertility symbol adopted and transformed by Jewish tradition into a symbol for life and Torah. The finials that ornament the end of the Torah scroll rods are called *rimmonim*, which is Hebrew for "pomegranates." When the waxing process was completed, the tablecloth was dyed a dark navy blue, but it could have been any strong color.

If you would rather do embroidery than batik, the linear quality of the design lends itself to a variety of different stitches. It could be done by hand or machine; the vest in Figure 75 was embroidered by machine.

36 The design was done using the Japanese technique called *mishima*, in which a white clay is painted over the entire surface upon which the design has been carved. The white clay is then scraped away from the raised surface of the plate, remaining only in the carved lines.

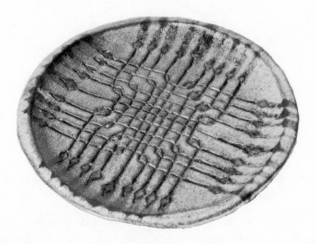

37 The interlocking-lamp design was embossed into this stoneware plate, using a wooden carving tool, while the clay is still soft.

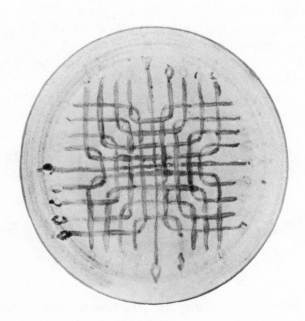

38 The lamp design was painted on this wheel-thrown plate, using liquid clay with cobalt oxide, which fires to a bright blue color.

39 This dish was made by draping a ⅜-inch slab of clay over part of an old divided serving dish. The edge of the clay was then folded over on itself and pinched into ridges, much as one seals the edge of a pie.

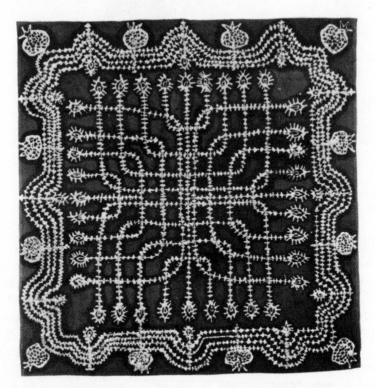

40 Dark blue batik tablecloth.

41 Papier-mâché Judith wine bottle.

The figure of Judith has inspired more writers, musicians, and artists than any other character in the Apocrypha. (Daniel is probably a close second.) As we have seen, she has often been used to decorate Hanukkah lamps, and she has been depicted on many Christian as well as Hebrew manuscripts. The cathedral at Chartres has a figure on the north portal of Judith praying, and in the Piazza della Signoria in Florence there is a bronze sculpture of Judith and Holofernes done by Donatello in the fifteenth century. Goya, during his Black Period, painted a very dramatic and haunting interpretation of Judith beheading the sleeping general. Since the custom of eating cheese foods at Hanukkah is attributed to Judith, a wine and cheese party provides a pleasant opportunity to pay tribute to her and to try Israeli wines and cheeses as well.

The wine bottle in Figure 41 was made by covering an ordinary commercial half-gallon wine bottle with papier-mâché, following the same process described on pages 104–5. The arms were made of thin rolls of newspaper taped in place. Holofernes' head was made of a folded wad of newspaper similarly held in place with masking tape. Judith's head was formed by wrapping a crumpled ball of newspaper with paper napkins and attaching it to the metal screw top of the bottle. A collar of cardboard was added to disguise the original shape and to suggest shoulders. After the several layers of papier-mâché had dried, heavy string was dipped in glue and added to her skirt, forming a relief design. She was painted with latex underpaint and acrylic colors, and then her hair—a hank of yarn—was glued in place. The bottle can be refilled with your favorite wine and, unless it is put in the dishwasher, will last for many Hanukkah parties.

MUSIC

No holiday celebration is complete without music. The first Hanukkah was celebrated by Judah and his men with "song and harps and lutes, and with cymbals" (I Macc. 4:54). Since the early celebration was modeled after Sukkot, it is likely that Psalms 113–18 (Hallel) were sung, and probably the Davidic Psalm of Dedication, Psalm 30, as well. The blessings for the lights are customarily sung rather than spoken, and throughout the centuries a body of hymns and folksongs has grown up for Hanukkah. These traditional songs can be found in a number of books and songsters distributed through most synagogues, religious schools, and Jewish centers.

Over the years I have collected records of Jewish music from different periods and countries, and our annual Hanukkah party is a wonderful opportunity to share these with friends. I have taped a potpourri of Jewish music, picking my favorites from various records. The tape is an interesting mixture of music with Yiddish, Ladino, Hebrew, Russian, English, and Arabic backgrounds. Because the story of Joseph and his brothers is the Torah portion read in the synagogue during the Hanukkah season, I have included on this tape parts of the rock musical *Joseph and the Amazing Technicolor Dreamcoat.**

*Scepter Records, New York.

Although it may not always appear so to outsiders, the most enjoyable music is that which we make ourselves. This year I was particularly pleased when my eldest son set the poem "Blessed Is the Match" to an American blues progression. The poem is by the martyred Hannah Senesh, who left Palestine during World War II to parachute behind enemy lines in an attempt to make contact with European Jews. She was captured and killed by the Nazis.

Blessed Is the Match

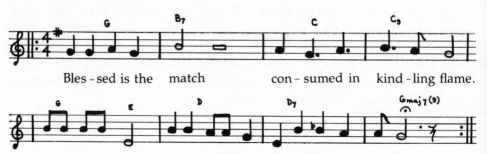

Bles - sed is the match   con - sumed in kind - ling flame.

Bles - sed is the flame that burns in the se - cret fast - ness of the heart.

> Blessed is the heart with strength to stop
> its beating for honor's sake
> Blessed is the match consumed
> in kindling flame.*

Putting the poem into a blues format expresses an element inherent in the poem itself, while making it more accessible to American teenagers.

*From *Hannah Senesh: Her Life and Diary* (New York, Schocken Books, 1972).

Celebrating
with Children

PROJECTS IN DIFFERENT MEDIA

Unlike some of the more somber holidays, Hanukkah is a holiday that is accessible to everyone regardless of age. The youngest children will respond to its festiveness and warmth, and even without comprehending their meaning, they will be fascinated with the lights. Depending on their age, they will get caught up in different parts of the history of Hanukkah and of the legends associated with it. Teenagers can comprehend and identify with the problems inherent in the meeting and mingling of Hellenism and Hebraism.

But whatever the level of comprehension, active participation in the preparations and celebration of the holiday will enrich its meaning. Children are sometimes so excited at the prospect of getting presents that the gift-giving aspect of the holiday can come to totally dominate it. Rather than suggest that they give gifts in return (which means even greater stress on presents), it is important to involve them in doing and making things which will add to their understanding of the meaning of Hanukkah while they are having a good time. As parents and teachers we enjoy doing things for them, but they can get a great deal from making their own Hanukkah party food, writing and directing their own dramatics (which are usually awful in a wonderful way), and making decorations for the religious school and home.

Several of these projects were made with and by children. Others in the book are adaptable to their skills and to the needs of classes and other groups. Projects for children's craft classes should produce objects that the child or his family can actually use and that they will genuinely find aesthetically pleasing or at least functional. For a child to make a Hanukkah menorah out of styrofoam and then to be told it is too inflammable to use it is a disheartening experience. He is unlikely to be inspired to go on to make anything else. Nothing is as discouraging to the child as bringing home a project he has made and being told how "nice" it is—only to find it in the trash a few days later.

The problem is a multifaceted one. Obviously we cannot keep every scrap of arts-and-crafts work our prolific children produce. Framing everything is out of the question; the cost would be prohibitive and the walls would soon collapse. Children are all known (at least by their adoring parents) to be creative, spontaneous geniuses. Indeed, the work done by them has a charm and intensity that seems to diminish as they get older. To expect the eleven-year-old to produce the spontaneous and "creative" work of the four-year-old is to ignore the way a pre-adolescent sees the world.

Children often lose interest in art after the very early grades, seeing it only as busywork. At the same time that the child is learning to read, we continue to treat his artistic creations with the same blanket enthusiasm that was perhaps suitable at two and three, when the child painted and drew his first recognizable people. We acknowledge the child's emerging questioning intellect in relation to other disciplines such as mathematics, music, and reading, and from the time the child begins to study these subjects, he is confronted with the reality of "right" and "wrong" answers, neatness, and the acquisition of usable skills. When a child learns that it isn't good enough to be "creative" with spelling, he becomes suspicious of an area of activity where everything is said by the adult world to be equally good, where definable standards are absent and technical skills rarely taught.

At an earlier period in history children worked alongside their parents and began to master carpentry, sewing, and other skills which served them in very good stead later in life. Today's children should be taught craft skills that will grow with them as they develop. In that way their projects will become more and more sophisticated as they reach maturity. Although the following projects are uncomplicated enough to be used in the elementary school classroom, I would like to encourage teachers and parents to help children explore more complex and time-consuming techniques, which might ultimately be more rewarding for them.

Paper Cuts

One type of decoration, commonly used throughout the Christmas season and perfectly suitable for Hanukkah as well, is the cut-paper snowflake. In Poland and Russia during the nineteenth and early twentieth centuries paper cuts similar to snowflakes were hung in windows to decorate for the spring holiday of Shavuot. They were cut into more curvilinear designs and were not called snowflakes but rather *roysalech* "little roses." Most examples of these and of the even more elaborate paper cuts made as *mizrahim*, Simhat Torah flags, and *ketubah* ornaments were destroyed during the Holocaust. Today Israeli schoolchildren are reviving the *roysalech* for Shavuot. Perhaps our children, along with us, could use some of the techniques and motifs from the traditional papercuts to make Hanukkah decorations. Figures 16 and 17 are examples of paper cuts that were reproduced as greeting cards. Both of them use a *hanukkiah* as the principal motif. The papercut in Figure 42 was done for Hanukkah but is based on the story of Daniel in the lions' den rather than on any of the more common Hanukkah symbols.

The Book of Daniel was composed by an unknown author during the period of the Maccabean revolt to strengthen and comfort the people who were suffering under the persecution of Antiochus. Although the characters and events are probably a mixture of fact and legend, the intention of the work is more important than its historicity. The moral of the stories is that people of sincere faith can resist temptation and triumph over adversity. Daniel's visions and prophecies are meant to teach that great political nations are powerful for only a brief period before they are consumed by still stronger nations; only the Kingdom of God will last forever, and the days to come will bring deliverance and glory to the oppressed.

The stories and visions in the Book of Daniel provide a great deal of potential visual material for Hanukkah projects. Daniel was condemned to be eaten by lions and thrown into their den as a result of a plot by the king's ministers, who found Daniel praying to God. The paper cut shows Daniel at peace with four rampant lions; a pair of angels hover above, symbolizing Daniel's faith and God's protective intervention.

To make a paper cut, begin by folding a sheet of paper in half—or in quarters for a more elaborate design or *roysale*. Draw half of the design in pencil on one side of the folded paper. Almost any kind of paper can be used—colored, white, or black; or even patterned paper and

42 Daniel and the Lions paper cut.

43   Paper-cut chains.

magazine photographs. Decide on your subject matter and pick two or three symbols to tell the story. Draw them as simply as possible; it is their silhouette rather than any internal detail that is important. As you draw the figures on the paper, try to get as much definition into the outside shape as possible, but always make sure that each form touches the others at enough points so that the whole thing won't fall into separate shapes when you begin cutting. Sometimes a little foliage helps to tie disparate shapes together.

Traditionally the folded paper with the design on it was tacked to a wooden board and cut out with the point of a sharp knife. I find that embroidery scissors do the job as well and are easier for me to handle. Sometimes for particular shapes I use cuticle scissors, and occasionally a hobby utility knife comes in handy. Remember as you cut to keep the shapes connected! With some practice you will be able to get more and more detail into your designs.

Paper cuts can also take the form of a long chain. These are nice to hang across the top of doorways, or very long ones can be assembled and hung across an entire room. Most of us cut strings of paper dolls when we were children; this is basically the same process. I have seen streamers using dreidels or stars, but it is more rewarding to do something less usual. The three paper-cut chains in Figure 43 were done by a seven-year-old, using motifs based on her reaction to parts of the Hanukkah story: elephants, soldiers, and little girls holding *hanukkiot*.

Printmaking

Printmaking offers many possibilities for making attractive cards, wrapping paper, and decorations. One of the most popular techniques used with children is that of potato printing. I sometimes think its popularity is based more on the novelty of using a vegetable to do artwork than on ease or aesthetics. For while it is possible to print using a carved potato or carrot to make a stamping block, there are other materials that are easier to carve, produce better prints, and last longer. But if nothing else is available, potatoes *can* be used to print from, and just because they are potatoes, it is fun. The menorah in Figure 44 was printed by

44 Potato-print menorah.

using a potato carved into a flower shape. After carving the potato, let it dry out a little so that it will accept the color. Block-printing ink or artists' oil paints can be used. Spread some on a flat surface (a sheet of glass with the edges taped makes an excellent palette), press the potato into the color, and then stamp it onto the paper, making any pattern you like. This print was done on translucent tracing paper so it could be hung in a window.

The print in Figure 45 was made by using a hobby utility knife to carve a menorah in the square end of an art gum eraser. This was inked on an ink-filled stamp pad and printed on rice paper for use as wrapping paper. It is easier to carve fine detail into an eraser than into a potato, and the eraser will not deteriorate if you do not finish all of your printing in one session.

Printing from styrofoam is a process that can be as simple or complex as you want it to be. The basic materials, styrofoam meat trays, are abundantly available. Try to get them from various supermarkets because they will often have different textures. The big ones steaks are packaged in are the most useful, but any size will do. Wash and dry them thoroughly before you begin. Use scissors and a hobby utility knife to cut the shapes you want. I was pleased with the various lions and angels in the Daniel paper cut and so decided to do a series of ten prints, using the same figures but different colors and arrangements.

After you have cut out the figures you want to use from the styrofoam sheets, additional detail can be added by pressing designs into the styrofoam. Anything that will leave an impression in the soft styrofoam can be used. These impressed details will remain as white lines or patterns when you print. For the colors, you can use block-printing ink to which a little linseed oil has been added or artist's oil paints. Put some ink into a palette and use a soft block-printing roller (available in hobby and art-supply stores) to roll an even coat of ink on the palette; this will help avoid streaks and splotches on the styrofoam. Then roll the color onto the styrofoam figure. You can get several colors on one figure by the careful use of several small rollers. The lions' heads are made from separate pieces of styrofoam so they can be more easily printed in colors different from those used for the bodies.

Pick up the inked figure carefully by the outer edges and place it inked side down where you would like it to print on the paper. Then use a *clean* roller to press the styrofoam very firmly against the paper. (If an extra clean roller is unavailable, place a thin sheet of paper over the

45 Menorah-stamped wrapping paper.

46 Daniel and the Lions styrofoam prints.

figure and press evenly and firmly with your hand. A rolling pin over a sheet of waxed paper could also be used.)

Gently peel back the styrofoam figure and admire your print! There will still be some ink left on the styrofoam, so it can be printed a second time, but the resultant print will be much fainter than the first one. By playing with faint and dark images, you can obtain interesting and unusual effects. If you want to make many copies of your print, you must re-ink the styrofoam in the same manner every time. The styrofoam will hold up much longer than you expect it to. It seems to get stronger as it absorbs the oil from the paint. But should a figure tear, it is simple enough to cut a duplicate from another meat tray.

Eleazer and the Elephant

Papier-mâché is an excellent medium for all ages above five. It can be used for everything from tiny trinkets to large elaborate sculpture or even furniture. It lends itself very well to three-dimensional interpretations of Hanukkah story material. These can be used as table decorations, or different episodes from the story could be depicted by a school class and all the parts arranged as a tableau.

The scene in Figure 47 depicts the attempt by Eleazer, one of Judah's brothers, to stab the warrior elephant he thought Antiochus' son was riding on in the battle lead by the Syrian General Lysias. Eleazer's intention was to crawl under the elephant and stab it in its soft underbelly, escaping as it fell to climb on the beast and kill the king's son. He didn't manage to get out in time and was crushed to death when the elephant fell on him. Eleazer was the first of the five brothers to die in battle.

The elephant and soldiers in Figure 47 were made by my daughter

47 Child's papier-mâché elephant with small figures.

when she was seven years old. They were done in four sessions of about one hour each. First the shape of the elephant was assembled, using a small balloon for the body and four pieces of cardboard tubes from a roll of paper toweling for the legs. The cardboard-tube pieces were attached to the balloon with masking tape. The head was formed from a long and narrow plastic bag stuffed with paper and twisted into a masking-tape-wrapped trunk. This was secured in place with more masking tape. If you don't have a balloon for the body, a stuffed plastic bag can be used here as well.

When the basic shape, or armature, is constructed, the first layer of papier-mâché is put on. Papier-mâché can be made with pulp of paper soaked in a paste mixture. I prefer, however, to use small torn pieces of newspaper, which are dipped into wallpaper paste to which a little white glue has been added. Children also seem to find this a satisfying way to work. Wallpaper paste can be bought in most hardware stores or from any store that sells wallpaper, but if it is not available, a mixture of flour, water, and salt makes a fine substitute. The paste mixture should be about the consistency of thin sour cream. The first layer of newspaper and paste can be fairly thick, but if the armature gets too wet, it might collapse. Allow the elephant to dry at least overnight before adding the ears, tower, and tusks. Drying can be hastened by putting the papier-mâché sculpture into an oven with only the pilot light on.

At the next session, ears and tower were cut from thin cardboard and taped to the elephant; tusks and tail were made from pipe cleaners and similarly attached. Another layer of paper and paste was applied, covering all the taped joints. Make certain the sculpture dries thoroughly before painting.

If you use a layer of white paper toweling as your final layer, you can avoid having to use a coat of white paint to cover the newsprint. White latex wall paint is very good to use if an undercoat is necessary. You can paint the decoration directly on the newsprint, but the colors will not be as brilliant as when there is white under them. Poster paint or acrylics are good for painting. A glossy varnish (acrylic for easy cleanup) is applied when all the paint has dried.

The little people in Figure 47 were made from pipe cleaners wrapped in masking tape and papier-mâché. These were dipped into the thick latex wall paint used for undercoating the elephant and then painted with acrylic colors. The lamp in Figure 12, dreidels in Figure 54, and bottle in Figure 41, as well as the elephant above, were all made with variations of the same simple papier-mâché process.

Banner Appliqué Workshop

The appliqué banner shown in Figures 48 and 49 was made with a group of teenagers at the Princeton Jewish Center. By the time young people have reached high school age, they have had a surfeit of art classes from which they bring home a weekly project for Mommy's admiration. A Jewish center should be a place where real things are made, not merely studied; the purpose of the workshop was to give the participants the experience of working as apprentices on a major undertaking. The concept of apprenticeship has been out of fashion in this country for a while, but it is happily beginning to return on a small scale among serious craftspeople.

The goal of the group was to produce in eight two- to three-hour sessions a 3-by-5-foot wall hanging that could ornament the center during the Hanukkah season. My additional intention was to see to it that as the students improved their appliqué and embroidery skills, they also learned something about the Hanukkah-related subject matter depicted in the banner and something about design.

Whether one makes such a banner with a group or alone, the basic procedure is the same. The hardest part is getting going; having once decided to do it, the idea begins to seem overwhelming. Decide on your subject matter, and with the various themes and symbols tucked in a corner of your mind, systematically break down the problems and decide one thing at a time. Determine the size and shape of the finished banner. How many helpers, how much time you have, and the place where it will eventually hang will help to determine the size and whether it will be a vertical or horizontal design. Pick a color palette, a group of related colors with which you want to work. The appliqué shown here was worked principally in earth and flame colors, because they seemed suitable to Hanukkah. One of the predominant motifs of this holiday is flame and light, and although fire is not specifically represented in the design, its color is present. Blue, particularly a bright cerulean, was used as an accent and to suggest the divine. There is a touch of blue in all the little scenes, and the amount of it increases at the top of the design, where "heaven" is implied with a "hand of God" reaching out from cloudlike shapes and a flying bird.

Once you have decided upon the colors you want to use, go directly to a fabric store or to your own collection of fabrics, and work with what is available in the palette you have chosen. If you spend time

48 Appliqué banner.

meticulously painting the colors you want for your design, you may be disappointed to find they do not exist in the fabrics you need. Use what is available, and build around it. When you have decided upon your colors, remove all other possibilities and stick to those you've selected. Limiting and tightening the range of color helps to produce a more integrated and controlled design.

Once the subject matter, size, and colors are decided, draw several small rough compositional sketches. These organizational sketches are helpful if they are kept to the general proportions you plan to work in. Since the finished appliqué was to be 3 by 5 feet, I measured off a number of rectangles that were 3 by 5 inches and some that were 6 by 10 inches and began to arrange the various symbols within those small shapes. These sketches are not meant to be definitive but rather to provide an idea of the overall composition and the relative sizes of the various parts. Small sketches were also done for some of the figures. After these preliminary sketches no more drawing was done; all further "sketching" was done directly with fabric or by cutting and tearing large pieces of paper into the needed shapes. These paper forms can then be used as patterns for cutting the shapes out of fabric.

Be patient with yourself in coming up with the overall design. Be prepared to spend many hours planning and rearranging. If you have a design from previous work you've done, don't be afraid to use it again. If you plagiarize from yourself often enough, it gets to be called style. The same Daniel and the Lions who appeared in the paper cut in Figure 42 reemerged in the prints in Figure 46 and appear once again in yet another technique in the appliqué in Figure 49. In designing this appliqué, I wanted to incorporate many of the stories and themes related to Hanukkah. I decided to use a large house shape, which could represent the rededicated Temple, as the means to organize the little vignettes I wanted to include. Within the Temple is the seven-branched Temple menorah. At the base are the five Hasmonean brothers and their father Mattathias; they have been arranged to spell out מכבי (Maccabee). One branch of the lamp frames Daniel with two lions; another shows Judith placing the head of Holofernes in a sack held by her maid. Above them hover two angellike forms, indicating that the deeds of both Daniel and Judith were accomplished with divine help. The crown at the top of the Temple was lightly stuffed with Dacron and has appliquéd to it the letter ש (shin) for "Shaday."

Since everyone in the group had at one time or another put up a

49 Details of the banner.

50 Labels on the back of the appliqué banner.

hem, a basic blind stitch was used almost throughout. Each person's way of sewing is as individual as handwriting, and we tried to make use of these individual variations by having the different people sew those parts where their particular style would do the most to enhance the overall effect. Because of the different levels of ability among the members of the group, it was important to get everyone to do a little bit all over the banner, giving it a uniform quality. The participants in the workshop each made a label with their Hebrew name on it, and these were sewn to the lining of the banner. They enjoyed making the labels as much as the banner.

HANUKKAH CELEBRATIONS IN SCHOOL

This chapter has been an attempt to provide some inspiration for Hanukkah activities in the home or with groups of people in synagogues, Sunday schools, and youth groups, but nowhere have I mentioned the problem of decorations for Hanukkah in the public schools. The reason for this is simple: I do not feel there should be any.

Growing up in the Bronx in an almost totally Jewish neighborhood, I went to a public school which was staffed almost entirely by Irish Catholics. We decorated the school immediately after Thanksgiving with everything from wreaths to crèches and images of the Holy Family. It never occurred to me then that Christmas was anything but a school phenomenon. It did not touch my internal or family life at all. I remember spending endless days sewing red-felt Christmas stockings and filling them with with candy to be sent to the Red Cross for distribution. I drew quantities of Christmas trees and Santa Clauses based on other pictures in books, since I had never seen a real Christmas tree and my mother didn't take me downtown on the subway to Macy's to see Santa Claus (television wasn't here yet). We did everything as much as possible in the proper Christmas spirit, for it was felt by our teachers that this was as good for us as the cod-liver oil our mothers gave us each morning. It is almost funny (if it weren't really so sad) to think of a roomful of Jewish children singing about the Virgin Birth and playing with dolls of the infant Jesus, under the tutelage of well-meaning teachers who had no idea of what went on in the Jewish homes in the neighborhoods in which they taught. In our apartment, for example, when I would bring home one of those Christmas drawings of a jolly Santa Claus and his bagful of goodies, no comment was made. Unlike most of my artwork, which was treasured, these just disappeared.

When Hanukkah came about the same season, no attempt was made at decorating the house. A small tin lamp was lit every night and sat on top of the refrigerator. Why there, I don't know. The refrigerator was in a sense a shrine in the kitchen. There was always a fresh starched and ironed scarf on it and a bowl of fruit or something nice, and then at Hanukkah the little lamp. I can't say there was a contrast with what went on in school. There can only be a sense of contrast if there is a relationship between the two activities. For me there was none. There were simply two parallel lives that never touched.

After my marriage, when my husband and I were posted at the American Embassy in Buenos Aires, my husband, as the most junior officer, was asked to run the embassy's Christmas party. He refused—first, because he felt it was inappropriate to use government funds and property to celebrate a religious holiday (though he would cheerfully help friends and colleagues celebrate at their homes), and second, because organizing a Christmas observance was against his beliefs as a Jew. We later discovered that reports of this incident had made their way into his file in Washington. Thus when we were transferred to Madrid and my young son, after just a few days at his new school, came home upset because the teacher wanted all the children to bring in Christmas ornaments to decorate a tree in every room, we had a terrible feeling of déjà vu.

Since the Madrid school was a private institution, the principle of separation of church and state was not involved. Nevertheless, I discussed the problem with the teacher, who ironically turned out to be a Jewish woman from New York. Her apologetic explanation was that even though Spanish observance of Christmas does not include the vast amounts of decorations and Christmas trees as we know them, the American School of Madrid was trying to give the children a total American education. Schools in the United States, she reminded me, always teach a Christmas unit at that time of year. She must have had the same teachers I'd had as a child! And she went on to show me the spelling book, with the unit for December devoted to a vocabulary full of Christmas-associated words. My ineffectual protest made, I gathered a few like-minded people and we began a Sunday school for the American Jewish children in Madrid.

Four years later, when we returned to America, we finally came face-to-face with the problem of Christmas-Hanukkah in the public schools. How subtle and complicated a problem it is! This time it was our second son who came home from school troubled because he was supposed to be making Christmas wreaths in his art class. We decided that the time had come to try to pursue the problem in a systematic fashion. Although we did speak to the children's teachers that year, we knew very well that each teacher was only a small—often totally unaware—participant in a nationwide pattern. Our decision was to begin working on the whole school system for the *following* season. Accordingly, as soon as Christmas was over, we wrote to the superintendent of schools to try to set up a meeting with the school board during the spring or summer, when feelings were not high, in order to lay plans for the coming year. The story of our local fight is not much different from those of other communities, complete with newspaper headlines reading, "SCROOGE WANTS TO TAKE SANTA OUT OF SCHOOL," and unpleasant phone calls; our living-room window is still cracked. It took two years and several school board hearings (one—ironically scheduled on the first night of Hanukkah—helped us enormously by pointing out the insensitivity of the majority culture) before we were really taken seriously and a new set of guidelines for teachers was drawn up for the school system.

The problem now was: What do you do with the children from Thanksgiving until Christmas? How do you decorate the classrooms and hallways? We had long ago rejected the idea of "equal time, equal space" for Hanukkah. Since our reasoning is that school is not the place for religious observance, we certainly did not want Hanukkah to be added as a second course to a meal we didn't want in the first place. We were joined by a good number of serious Christians who felt that the schools were trivializing an important religious event, that the commercialization of religion which is so prevalent in America had crept into the schools as well. They wanted Christmas out of the schools in order to keep it sacred. Our opposition so often came from people who gave their children little or no religious background and felt that what they got in school was "good" for them.

Fortunately, the committee responsible for special exhibitions in the schools was doing some creative thinking at the time. They reasoned that since the winter is a time for holidays in all religions, the school time could well be spent in studying comparative religion on various levels. There is a big difference between learning about a religion and being compelled to celebrate its festivals. An exhibit was organized around the broad theme of the world's religions and was initially set up in the largest school in town. It was an ambitious and very successful undertaking. All the art teachers and their students built life-size tableaux, mainly using corrugated cardboard, discarded boxes, and lots of paint. The tableaux included sections of a mosque, a Hindu temple, a Shinto altar, and a replica of a synagogue *bima*. There were Catholic and Buddhist altars, as well as a nondeistic section explaining the humanistic approach to life, which finds religion in nature and in the humanity of mankind. The cost in materials was about two hundred dollars. The display was enriched by valuable artifacts that were loaned to the

51

schools by institutions and individuals in the community. Thus the Catholic display had magnificently embroidered church vestments, and the "mosque" displayed an exquisite illuminated Koran. Seven artists were invited to make prints based on the theme of the Golden Rule as interpreted by the different religions. It was fascinating to every-one — children, parents, and teachers — to see how subtle differences exist between one religion and another in the concepts of care and consideration, which are themes common to all religions. I did an etching (Figure 51), based on photographs from World War II, which combined the phrases "Love your neighbor as yourself" (Lev. 19:18) and "Whatever is hateful to you, do not do unto another" (Hillel). My colleagues each took quotations from Christianity, Buddhism, Hinduism, Islam, Confucianism, and Sikhism, which, though similar, all emphasized different facets of this basic tenet. The prints were bought by the Parent-Teachers Association Council and traveled to all the schools in the area, along with other parts of the show. The exhibit was shown on weekends to Sunday school groups.

I've described this exhibit at length because I feel that it was a commendable and worthwhile way of meeting a difficult problem. Displays like this, which are truly educational in value, can be undertaken every year. They need not be as elaborate as the one described, which was in the nature of a pilot project, showing many possibilities. The only caution that must be made is that the exhibit should be prevented from deteriorating into "Christmas Around the World," thereby portraying Hanukkah and all the midwinter festivals of other religious groups as though they were mere variations of the Nativity story.

Games

ince ancient times Jews have enjoyed games and sports similar to
those of the people around them. Rabbinic attitudes toward these
diversions have varied from flatly condemnatory to allowing con-
gregationally sponsored games of chance to raise funds for the
synagogue. The fact that over the centuries there has been so much
discussion and legislation about them indicates that in spite of frequent
rabbinic disapproval, ordinary people continued to amuse themselves
with games. This interaction between rabbinic legality and human
nature has developed into the general Jewish attitude that gambling for
personal gain (especially by professionals, who might very well fall into
the temptation to defraud the innocent) is to be frowned upon, whereas
playing for amusement—especially those games that involve skill rather
than luck and that encourage fellowship among the players—is not
disparaged. One of the principal reasons gambling was condemned was
that it was felt that participants were oblivious to *yishuv shel olam* (the
welfare of the world), which they would be promoting if they were using
the time misspent in gambling on a profession, trade, or study. However, since the Middle Ages the long winter nights of Hanukkah
particularly have traditionally been spent in playing games with family
and friends, thereby promoting domestic serenity. Thus over the centuries heavy gambling and betting were strongly discouraged, but it became
customary to play games in association with various holidays.

Both Hanukkah and Purim originated at about the same time, but
because of Hanukkah's long quiet period, there are many more illustrations of Purim celebrations than there are of Hanukkah pastimes. Aside
from those that simply show the lighting of a Hanukkah lamp, with few

52 Turn-of-the-century postal greeting card based on Hermann Junker's painting of a Hanukkah evening in the home of a nineteenth-century Jew. Printed in Frankfurt. Reproduced by permission of the Jewish Theological Seminary of America.

exceptions most paintings and prints of Hanukkah depict scenes such as the one in Figure 52. Junker's painting is very similar to a domestic Hanukkah scene painted by Moritz Oppenheim in 1880. Both show the candles aglow in the window while the family is absorbed in a variety of games, including chess and cards. J. G. Puschner's plate for Paul Christian Kirchner's *Jüdisches Ceremonial* (Nuremberg, 1734) shows a similar scene more than a century earlier, which also has children on the floor playing with dreidels (this curious print also confirms the fact that lamps suspended from the ceiling were commonly used for Hanukkah in Germany).

Since game-playing has been so much a part of Hanukkah custom, it has been said to have originated during the Maccabean struggle as a means of subterfuge. After Antiochus outlawed Torah study, pious

Jews would keep a dreidel or deck of cards on the table along with the holy books. If the group was discovered by Antiochus' soldiers, they could pretend they had only gathered to gamble.

Dreidels

The most popular Hanukkah game is a put-and-take game played with a spinning top called a dreidel. Although we think of it as *the* prototypi-

53 Dreidels with *gelt*, raisins, and nuts.

cal Jewish toy, it is but a variation of the spinning top some historians believe to have developed into a plaything from the spindle-whorl used for spinning thread in ancient Japan. With the exception of riddles and intellectual word and number games, Jews through the ages have rarely originated their own games; they usually adapted games played in the surrounding culture to their own needs. Like other folkloric customs, games seldom change their seasons. It may very well be that tops were played with by Jews during the Graeco-Roman period. We know with more certainty, however, that the four-sided dreidel with which we are familiar became common as a Hanukkah amusement among Ashkenazic Jews at the beginning of the Middle Ages.

The dreidel has a Hebrew letter on each of its four sides: נ (*nun*), ג (*gimel*), ה (*he*), ש (*shin*). They stand for Yiddish words meaning "take" (*nem*) or "nothing" (*nisht*), "give" (*gib*), or "all" (*gantz*), "half" (*halb*), and "put" (*shtel*). Greater dignity was given to the dreidel by interpreting the letters to stand for the phrase *Nes gadol haya sham* ("a great miracle happened there"). In Israel dreidels are made with the letter *pe* replacing *shin*; the substitution signifies that in Israel "a great miracle happened *here*" (*po*). Thus a simple game is transformed into a reminder of the Hanukkah story and of the modern miracle of reborn Israel.

The game is played by having each player contribute an agreed-upon amount of nuts or candy or whatever to the kitty, and then spinning the dreidel in turn, paying the penalty indicated by the letter that is on top when the dreidel falls. If the player spins *nun*, nothing happens and he passes; *gimel*, the player gets all that is in the pot (in which case everybody contributes to make up a new kitty); *he*, the player gets one-half of the kitty; *shin*, the player must put into the kitty whatever forfeit has been agreed upon when the game began. The game ends when one player has won everything from the others or when all have had enough (the winner being the player who has won most).

Since even in Yiddish the meanings are sometimes different, in my family we use the letters to represent English words ("nothing," "get," "half," "share"); this makes it easier for even the youngest children to remember the rules of the game. Another form of the game makes use of the numerical values of the letters: *nun* = 50, *gimel* = 3, *he* = 5, *shin* = 300.

Dreidels have been made out of diverse materials, including very elaborate ones from silver and ivory. Wood continues to be a favorite material, both for expert carvers and today's home craftsman with power tools. The dreidel is primarily a children's toy, and children love to make their own. Yemeni children made a top for Hanukkah called a *duame* from nutshells, and the *heder* students in the Pale of Settlement made metal dreidels by pouring lead into four-part carved wooden forms. A delightful folksong grew up about these lead dreidels, which begins with the couplet:

Ikh bin a kleyner dreidel	I am a little dreidel
Gemakht bin ikh fun blay	I am made out of lead

The melody is so charming that the song is now popularly sung in an English version in many places in America. The English, however, probably in the interest of rhyme, substitutes "clay" for "lead," giving the misleading impression that clay dreidels are traditional and easy for children to make. Despite the song, the reverse is true: clay dreidels tend to be heavy and breakable, and they spin poorly.

Simple dreidels can be made even by young children from household discards such as egg cartons and wooden spools, using dowels for handles. An adult will have to cut the dowel into appropriate lengths (2 to 3½ inches depending on the size of the spool or carton), but the children can sharpen them with a pencil sharpener to provide the point for spinning. The dowel is held in place with an all-purpose white glue.

54 This dreidel is the basic egg carton lettered with felt-tip pens.

55 Beads, thumbtacks, acrylic paints, and colored nail polish were used to decorate spools and papier-mâché dreidels.

If it is too loose in the spool, a little plastic wood filler can be used. Use sandpaper to define and flatten four sides of the spool, or it may roll away after spinning. The smallest dreidel in Figure 55 uses eight thumbtacks to form the corners instead of sanding. You might consider making a dreidel that has the English words for the game along with the Hebrew letters. Or use the whole Hebrew phrase *nes gadol haya sham*.

Maccabees versus Syrian-Greeks Chess Set

We know from literary sources as well as from early prints and paintings showing Hanukkah domestic scenes that since the Middle Ages chess has been a popular game for long winter evenings. In spite of occasional rabbinical injunctions against it, chess has been enjoyed by Jews for a very long time. One legend even attributes the invention of the game to King Solomon.

It would be nice to believe this, but reputable historians of the game trace its origins to India, where it developed about fifteen hundred years ago. In their early forms the pieces represented elephants, chariots, and foot soldiers. The piece we know today as the bishop was then an elephant, which accounts for the two tusklike lines found on the bishops hat in many standard chess sets. The game was played centuries ago in China, India, and Persia. With the Arab invasion, the game traveled to Spain, and from Spain to the rest of Europe nine hundred years ago. It was in medieval Europe that chess assumed the familiar form of today's game.

It is not surprising that even though the Moslems and the Catholic

56 Maccabees versus Syrian-Greeks.

Church both tried unsuccessfully to stamp out chess, they met with little success. Among the Jews it has been generally accepted as a respected intellectual pastime. A story told about the eleventh-century chief rabbi of Mainz relates that he was playing chess with the pope and after a while recognized him as his son who had disappeared years before.

Chess sets have been made in many styles and materials. Many of the sets one sees may be made in Oriental or Napoleonic style but will have both sides identical, except for color. Making a Hanukkah set gave me the opportunity to have the two sides in genuine opposition to one another—the whites as Maccabees and the darks as Syrian-Greeks—emphasizing some of the differences between the two sides. I trust you will forgive the few small liberties I have taken with historical accuracy in the interest of the game and of design.

Before beginning any of the individual pieces, all the clay needed for the entire set was wedged (kneaded) and the relative sizes of the pieces were roughed out in clay cubes, cylinders, rectangles, and cones. This was done because I knew the whole set could never be finished in a single day (it took about six, including glazing), and the pieces shrink a great deal as they dry. The castles were basically 2-inch cubes of wet clay, the pawns were cylinders 2½ inches tall and 1½ inches wide, the knights were rectangles 2 inches by 2½ inches, the bishops were 3½-inch-tall cylinders, the queens were 4-inch tall cone shapes, and the kings were 4-inch tall rectangles. All these assorted lumps were covered with damp paper towels and wrapped in plastic; the different pieces of clay were removed as needed.

Because they are the simplest pieces and I wanted all four to be the same (since the Maccabees and the Syrian-Greeks were fighting over the same terrain), all the castles were made first. The pawns were done next. The Greek army was very well equipped. Using photos of ancient Greek pottery as a guide, I modeled my Greek pawns with helmets and shields over togalike clothes. The Jews, on the other hand, were basically an ill-equipped peasant army. Until they began to capture enemy equipment, their weapons consisted mainly of farm implements. The Maccabean pawns therefore carry only pitchforks. All the "hair" on the Jewish chess pieces was made by squeezing a small amount of clay through a garlic press and "gluing" the resultant clay threads in place with a mixture of vinegar and clay. To make them look more Jewish, I made them each wear a tiny yarmulke (skullcap). This has no historical

57 Kings and queens; opposing soldiers.

validity as far as I know. The yarmulke, as the typical Jewish head covering, is a relatively recent tradition.

The knights were done next, and again the difference in equipment was stressed, with the Greek cavalry carrying shields and wearing helmets, whereas the Jewish horsemen have only sticks to carry. It is unlikely that the Maccabees had horses at the beginning of their struggle, but they probably captured them along with other equipment from the enemy whenever they were victorious in battle.

Because of the religious nature of the Maccabean struggle, the bishops are as different from one another as possible. The Maccabean "bishop" is wearing the breastplate of the Temple high priest and his beard and yarmulke are meant to give him a spiritual look. I wanted the Greek "bishop" to embody what was religiously abhorrent to the Jews. To that end, he carries a sacrificial animal under one arm. Rather than have him as a saintly-looking figure, I gave him the furry legs of a Greek mythological creature.

The Greek queen is meant to suggest a fertility figure, while the Jewish queen is the brave Judith of Bethulia. Each king is seated on his throne. The Jewish throne is decorated with incised menorahs, which the Hasmoneans established as the national emblem of Judea and which are today the national emblem of reborn Israel. The Greek throne is decorated with a Classical Greek key design. The Greek king holds a sword, suggesting that his rule is through armed force, whereas the Jewish king sits relaxed on his throne. This is not entirely accurate, since as we have seen, the Maccabees weren't exactly pacifists.

The chessmen were finished with a special-formula glaze developed for me by a ceramicist friend. After much experimentation on test pieces, we were both happy with the resultant glaze, which remains clear and glossy when thinly applied and becomes very white when it collects in grooves and crevices. The same glaze was used on the dark pieces over an undercoat of dark green clay. The faces and arms were protected during glazing by a coat of wax applied carefully with a fine brush. The wax resists the glaze and later burns away in the kiln, leaving the clay bare on the previously waxed areas. The pieces were fired to stoneware temperatures in an electric kiln.

If you do not have ceramic facilities easily available but would still like to make a Hanukkah chess set, consider making the pieces of the self-hardening clay sold in hobby shops, of papier-mâché (which would have to be weighted), or of carved and painted plaster of Paris or wood.

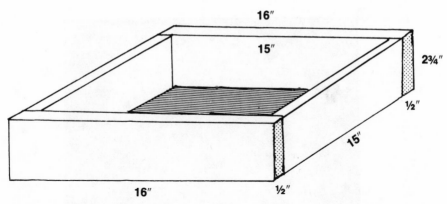

58 The basic chess box.

The wooden box was made of plywood and pine. I wanted it to be as unmistakably designed for Hanukkah as the chessmen, so I decorated it with the same quotation from the Shabbat Hanukkah Haftorah portion which was used for the needlepoint on page 76 and the *mizrah* on page 75. In this case, however, no English is used, and since the phrase is being used to decorate a totally secular object, I followed the custom of substituting the words *Ha-Shem* ("the Name") for the Hebrew *Adonay* ("Lord"). To avoid overcrowding the letters I eliminated the last two words, "of Hosts." Thus, the quotation from Zechariah on the chess box says: לא בחיל ולא בכח כי אם־ברוחי אמר ה' "Not by might, nor by power, but by my spirit, saith *Ha-Shem*."

The bottom of the box is a 15-inch square of ½-inch-thick plywood. The sides were made of ½-inch pine boards, which are sold by lumber yards in various widths. I used what is called a 3-inch wide pine plank (it really measures 2 and three-quarter inches). As Figure 58 indicates, the sides were attached to form a butt joint at the corner rather than a miter. Therefore two of the side pieces are 16 inches long and two 15 inches long. The finished box is a 16-inch square. The sides were attached with contact cement and finishing nails.

The letters were cut from paper-thin walnut veneer, which is sold in most lumberyards and some hardware stores in 2-inch wide rolls; it is very easy to work with. Think of it as if it were paper or fabric; draw the shapes with a pencil and cut them out with scissors. The letters were designed to fit the 2-inch width of the walnut strip. Before assembling the box, the letters were glued to each side with white glue, weighted, and allowed to dry thoroughly overnight.

59 The Jewish king, showing the beard made by forcing clay through a garlic press.

Compartments for the individual chess pieces were made by gluing three 15-inch lattice strips as shelves across the width of the box and then subdividing these shelves with additional short pieces of lattice stripping. Rectangles of felt were cut and glued to the bottom of the box to pad the ceramic pieces.

The lid of the box serves as the chess board. It was made from a 17-inch wide pine plank. It could also have been made from plywood, but then the sides would have had to be covered in some special way. The pine board may very well warp one day, and when it does, I will replace it with a framed plywood board. The alternate light and dark squares were made from the same 2-inch wide veneer as the letters, using walnut for the dark squares and birch veneer for the light squares. They were glued to the board with white glue, covered with paper, and weighted under many pounds of books until they were thoroughly dry. I glued four strips of lattice 1 inch in from each edge on the underside of the board. This was then covered with a 17-inch square of felt, glued in place. The lattice and the felt make the lid sit snugly on the box and hold the chess pieces in place when the box is being moved around. The box and lid were finished with a semi-gloss varnish.

Cards

Although chess has over the centuries established itself as a "respectable" game, the Jewish attitude toward card-playing remains much more ambiguous. This may be because cards have often been used to read into the future and therefore have taken on magical connotations or because cards are often played for personal gain rather than for simple amusement. Nevertheless, since the fifteenth century many a long winter's evening has been passed in Jewish households playing cards.

When my mother was a child in Poland, card games played at Hanukkah time used either ordinary decks of cards or cards that were made by the older children and called *kvitlakh;* a special "bank for the poor" was set aside from the winnings. In Mea Shearim, the ultra-orthodox area of Jerusalem, a Hanukkah card game is sold in book and toy stores; it has some "educational" value because the cards have the requirements for Hanukkah observance on them, but it is basically a game of sets, and each player tries to complete a collection of a particular group of cards in order to win.

A chess set is rather an ambitious undertaking, but a deck of cards can easily and inexpensively be made in an afternoon. It can be done by an individual or as a group project, with everyone making his own designs. Or the various stamps can be made by different individuals and then shared.

I modeled my deck of cards after commercially available playing cards, substituting Hanukkah symbols for the ordinary four suits. Instead of hearts, diamonds, clubs, and spades, I have used *hanukkiot* and dreidels for the black suits and pitchers and *magen Davids* for the red suits.

As with an ordinary deck, each of the four suits has thirteen cards, numbered from 1 to 10, a jack, queen, and king. It amuses me to think of a Queen of Dreidels, a King of Lamps, a ten of Stars, or a Jack of

Pitchers. Any ordinary card game can be played with this set. The favorite at our house is Go Fish. In commercial sets the value of the card is indicated by a number as well as by the motif of the suit. In the interests of simplification I decided to eliminate these numbers, and I find that the deck is just as easy to play with. Although it is possible to stamp the motifs on the cards in any pattern as long as one has the required number of symbols, I followed the patterns on ordinary cards, thus making the set familiar and the value of each card more easily recognized.

It was easy to decide on lamps and dreidels as the motifs for two of the suits. The other two were somewhat more difficult and need a bit of explaining. I could have used a hammer, which is the symbol associated with Judah the Maccabee, or an elephant or a single candle or a flame. But I wanted four that fit easily into the square shape at the end of the art gum erasers that were carved to make stamps and that did not require a lot of detail in order to be fully realized. I decided to use the *magen David* because although not specifically a Hanukkah symbol —and indeed not very old as a Jewish symbol—it is now commonly accepted as *the* Jewish symbol, as the cross is for Christians and the crescent for Moslems. While the six-pointed star has a long history as a magical symbol and appears with great frequency on architectural remains of previous centuries (more often than not on non-Jewish buildings), it is really in this century that the Star of David has been totally accepted as emblematic of the Jewish people. It was used as the central motif of the Zionist flag at the first Zionist Conference in 1897. When the Nazis tried to make it into a badge of shame, it became instead a sign for martyrdom and nationalism.

Although we do not often think of a pitcher as a common Hanukkah symbol, it has been one for centuries, connoting the single legendary cruse of oil found by the Maccabees. On the Hanukkah lamp shown in Figure 4, there is a small brass pitcher hanging in balance to the *shammash* position; it serves no function except as a reminder of the miracle of the oil. Such lamp decorations were not at all uncommon,and it is enjoyable to find and reuse symbols and motifs which have been out of fashion for a while.

In commercial decks of cards the kings, queens, and jacks will be somewhat different in each of the four suits. Those figures are ordinarily the most colorful, combining red and black and often yellow as well. The deck of cards I made is very simple, and the same king, queen, and

60 Playing cards.

61 The four suits.

jack serve all four suits, both red and black. Those more ambitious might choose to vary the royal figures or to elaborate them with the addition of more color. This might be done with felt-tip pens rather than by more printing, with which it is difficult to get too many colors superimposed at exactly the right places.

The materials needed are commonly available in most five-and-ten cent stores or stationery stores. I used 6 sheets of thin 11-by-14-inch poster board, each of which was cut in 12 cards. This was more than enough for the 52 cards of the deck and the trial cards and mistakes. Each card measures about 2¾ by 4⅞ inches. You will need 3 or 4 rectangular art gum erasers and two stamp pads, one black and one red. A pencil eraser or two can be cut into small additional shapes if desired. A sharp

62   The king and the partially printed queen.

knife or razor blade is needed to cut the design into the eraser. I find a hobby utility knife easiest to handle for this, since it is shaped very much like a pencil.

The erasers can be carved on all sides, but one must be careful not to cut away the edge of the design from the surface adjoining the one being carved. Printing is very simple and goes very quickly. One must re-ink the eraser stamp for each print and press it evenly and firmly to the card. My only word of caution in making these playing cards is to tell you to avoid overperfectionism. The process is so pleasant and simple that with very little effort a handsome game can be made. Don't waste unnecessary efforts in measuring or trying to line up the motifs with perfect spacing. From time to time an unwanted corner of the eraser will also print. Usually this will not matter at all and simply adds to the charm of the whole.

The royal figures are made by cutting into the long surface of the eraser for part of the figure and then adding a part cut from a separate part of the eraser. In the case of the king, his crown was made with an ordinary pencil eraser that had been cut to form a triangle. To print the royal family, draw a light pencil line down the center of the card in both directions and print each figure twice, once inverted, once right side up.

To store the cards you can use a box of the right size, if you have one, and cover it with paper printed with the stamps; if not, a box can be simply constructed from shirt cardboard, then covered.

After finishing the deck of cards, I used the stamps to make patterns on shelf paper and Japanese rice paper. This became my gift wrap; this time I used a purple stamp pad (Figure 45).

Jigsaw Puzzle

Puzzles have been a popular amusement at Hanukkah time for many centuries. They were not the jigsaw kind shown here but rather elaborate riddles and word and number games often based on *gematria*, which is a system of defining words and phrases by the numerical value of their Hebrew letters. Sometimes substitutions of other letter combinations were made in order to come up with semimystical, often humorous, meanings. These arithmetic, linguistic, and philosophical riddles, invented especially for Hanukkah, were called *katowes* (jests) and were designed so that the answer to them would be forty-four, the total number of candles burned during Hanukkah.*

The puzzle shown here does not involve complicated mental gymnastics. It was made from a photograph of my husband and daughter lighting the *hanukkiah*. If you don't have a suitable photograph for a Hanukkah puzzle, you could use a magazine illustration or a child's drawing or painting or one of your own. You will also need two pieces of Masonite that are 2 inches larger in both horizontal and vertical dimensions than the picture (the finished size of this puzzle is 13 by 16 inches, the photo was 11 by 14 inches), a double-face self-stick photographic mounting card the same size as the illustration (or photographic mounting cement if you prefer), all-purpose contact cement, and paint with which to decorate the frame.

Cut two 1-inch strips across the width of one of the pieces of Masonite and two 1-inch strips from along the remaining lengthwise edge. This will make the Masonite the same size as your picture and give you four pieces to frame it with (two 1 by 13 inches and two 1 by 14 inches). Use contact cement to glue these strips onto the second piece of Masonite along its outer edges. As you cut the puzzle pieces, you can place them in the prepared frame.

*There is also an old recipe for a *katowes* cake in which the number of ingredients totals forty-four.

Follow the manufacturer's directions for the particular photo-mounting product you have purchased, and attach your picture to the remaining trimmed sheet of Masonite. Use a pencil to lightly draw the shapes of the Hanukkah letters as illustrated or phrases and symbols of your own invention. I didn't want to cut into the faces, so they were made into heart shapes; I also left the candle intact, forming an enlarged flame shape at the top. The puzzle was then cut apart, using a lightweight table scroll saw. A hand coping saw could have been used, but I find this table-model saw, which is available through most hobby shops, as versatile and easy to operate as an electric sewing machine or kitchen mixer. It has been used for a number of projects in this book, and even young children (five years and up) can use it because it has a very safe finger guard.

After the puzzle has been cut, place a sheet of cardboard over it and turn it upside down out of the frame while you paint. Since the photo I used was a black-and-white one, I painted the frame a bright, cheerful red.

63 The puzzle pieces that are shaped into the Hebrew letters for Hanukkah, as well as the initial letter H, have been removed.

Pin the Shammash *on the* Hanukkiah *Appliqué*

At every birthday party I ever went to as a child, we played "pin the tail on the donkey," so when I needed a game for a children's Hanukkah party years ago, it was natural and easy to substitute a Hanukkah lamp for the donkey and candles for tails. The first games I made were of paper, but they became torn and shabby almost immediately. I decided to make one from a durable fabric, which would last for years and be pretty enough to keep up throughout the holiday, for my daughter to play with as she likes whenever she brings a friend home after school.

The game shown in Figure 64 was made of felt. Felt comes in a wide variety of colors, is strong, and does not need to have the edges turned under to prevent raveling. Since it is so often used for craft work, it is sold in small squares and rectangles of various dimensions as well as by the yard. To make the appliqué shown here, it is more economical to purchase the fabric for the lamp and flames in small pieces. For the background, you will need a 20-by-30 inch piece of dark brown felt; the rest was cut from 18-by-9-inch rectangles.

Yellow was used for the outer curve of the lamp, the *shammash*, 2 flames, and the base. Cut 2 of the J-shaped pieces, which are 2 inches wide. The horizontal leg is 9 inches long; the vertical part is 14½ inches tall. From the fabric left over from the inside curve of the J, cut for the base 1 curved piece 12 inches wide and 4½ inches at its highest point. Also cut 2 diamond-shaped flames. A strip 2 by 16 inches was used for the *shammash*.

Orange felt was cut for 4 vertical strips, each 1½ inches wide and 14½ inches long; 1 horizontal strip, 2 by 17 inches; 4 diamond-shaped flames; and a curved shape on the base cut from a 9-by-3½-inch rectangle. The curved piece is 2½ inches wide.

Bright pink was used for 2 vertical strips, 1½ by 14½ inches; 2 horizontal strips, 2 by 17 inches, 2 diamond-shaped flames; and the 1-inch-wide central strip on the base. This curved piece was cut from a rectangle 7½ by 3 inches.

Cut extra diamonds from all three colors with which to play the game.

Arrange the felt pieces on the background as shown in Figures 64 and 65, weaving the different colored strips over and under. Pin carefully to keep the lines and spaces even and straight. Red cotton

64 Children playing "pin the *shammash* on the *hanukkiah.*" The finished size of the game is 20 by 28 inches.

orange   pink   yellow

65 The pieces for the appliqué.

pearl embroidery thread was used with a simple running stitch to secure the pieces to the background fabric. Be careful when sewing to maintain the woven effect. Sew only along those edges that show. Fold a 2-inch hem under at the top of the background piece and sew a line of running stitches 1 inch below the fold, forming a pocket that enables the banner game to be hung on a rod if desired.

Any color combination you like can be substituted for the one I have used. I have described this one in order to emphasize the point that it is possible, and desirable, to make Jewish decorations in color combinations other than the overused blue and white.

Board Game

While specific athletic games are not associated with the celebration of Hanukkah, it is interesting to note that the international Jewish Olympics event that is held in Israel every four years is called the Maccabiah. The first Maccabiah was held in Tel Aviv in 1932. It was an outgrowth of the worldwide sports organization called Maccabi,* dedicated to physical fitness, which developed in the last decade of the nineteenth century in Europe. In Israel an annual torch relay is held bringing fire from Modi'in to light a *hanukkiah* in Jerusalem. An article in the *Jerusalem Post* during Hanukkah, 1974, described a relay sponsored by Maccabi in which a torch was carried to an El Al plane at Lod airport and then transported to New York City, where it was met by an American member of the organization. The torch (which had been extinguished on the plane) was then used to light an American Hanukkah lamp.

Many board games are often nothing more elaborate than a race from one point to another. A number of years ago when my boys were small, I made a Hanukkah game for them based on the idea of a competitive race from Modi'in to Jerusalem. They used their own toy soldiers, and a dreidel was used to determine the moves to be made. A drawing of this game is shown in Figure 66; it can be enlarged using the grid method and drawn or painted in color on heavy cardboard, Masonite, or wood. For older children you might want to use a reasonably accurate map of Israel as the game board. A more elaborate undertaking would be to make the game board as three-dimensional as possible, with perhaps wooden shapes to indicate the mountainous terrain. Rather than using ordinary toy soldiers, you might want to make game pieces of ceramic, papier-mâché, or wood.

The rules of the game are printed on the board. It is played by each player spinning the dreidel in turn. *Nun* נ means advance two spaces, *gimel* ג means advance three spaces, *he* ה means advance five spaces, and *shin* ש means retreat two spaces. If the player lands on an occupied space, he must retreat two spaces. If the player lands on the space marked Prisoner-of-War Camp, he can escape if another player lands there and is willing to free him; then they both get away free. If not, the second captive only has to retreat two spaces. While imprisoned, the P.O.W. has two spins of the dreidel per turn. If he succeeds

*Official name: World Maccabi Union.

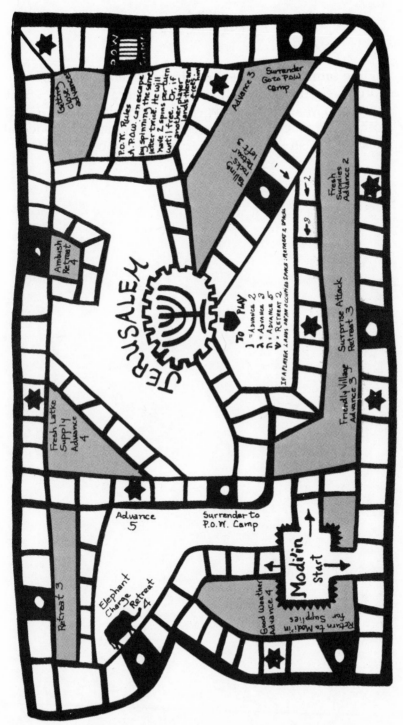

66 Hanukkah board game: the race from Modi'in to Jerusalem.

in spinning the same letter twice, he is free. All along the route some of the boxes involve penalties, such as "enemy encampment; retreat one space," "return to Modi'in for supplies," or "surprise attack; retreat two spaces"; others provide rewards, such as "level stretch; move ahead three spaces" or "fresh supply of *latkes*; advance four spaces."

Gifts

Banks for Hanukkah Gelt

It is customary to give presents on Hanukkah, mainly to children. But at various periods in different places the holiday provided an opportunity to bestow gifts upon a particular segment of the community. Thus in Eastern Europe teachers as well as students often received Hanukkah *gelt* (money), and among the Sephardim of Salonica, gifts of clothing and useful household items were traditionally given to newlyweds at Hanukkah, whereas children received candy and money. Giving gifts on Hanukkah is not, as is sometimes implied, merely imitative of Christmas. Both customs undoubtedly originate from a similar human desire to add joyousness to the somber days of winter, each religion explaining its traditional gift-giving by relating it to the origins of its respective holiday.

Although today all manner of presents are exchanged at Hanukkah, the traditional gift is that of *gelt*. When I was a child I received Hanukkah *gelt* from my parents and the few relatives who visited our apartment sometime during the holiday and drank a glass of tea in the kitchen. I very rarely got a whole dollar; usually it was just a few coins. Nevertheless, they were very important to me—not only for what they would buy but because I understood them to be symbolic reminders of the coins struck by the Hasmoneans when they achieved political independence.

Today we are all harassed by voluminous advertising, particularly at this time of year. My husband and I have experimented with various

67   Elephant banks.

"systems" of giving Hanukkah presents to our children. One year I look back upon with particular horror was the time we decided to give each child a different gift each night. That meant a total of twenty-four objects. Aside from financing this venture, the problems of jealousy and parity that surfaced every evening all but destroyed the simple joyousness with which we wanted to approach the holiday. The happiest solution we have found is to give the children gifts on the first and last nights of Hanukkah and some small trinket the evening we light the fourth or fifth candle. Whichever system we follow, we always give the children coins. On the first night of Hanukkah they each get one penny, the second night, two, and so forth, until after receiving eight on the last night they each have a total of thirty-six pennies. So while we do still occasionally let the presents get out of hand, the copper coins serve as a link to the older tradition of Hanukkah *gelt* and therefore to the Maccabees. I like the fact that the children receive *thirty-six* coins: The numerical sum of the Hebrew letters for the word life חי equals eighteen. Therefore to my way of thinking, thirty-six is doubly lucky.

In order to accommodate these coins and any other Hanukkah *gelt* the children receive from grandparents and relatives, I made them each a ceramic Hanukkah *gelt* bank. If you do not have ceramic facilities available, you might want to make elephant banks from papier-mâché, forming the body over a small balloon, as was done with the warrior elephant decoration in Figure 47.

For obvious reasons, a piggy bank is unsuitable for Hanukkah *gelt*.

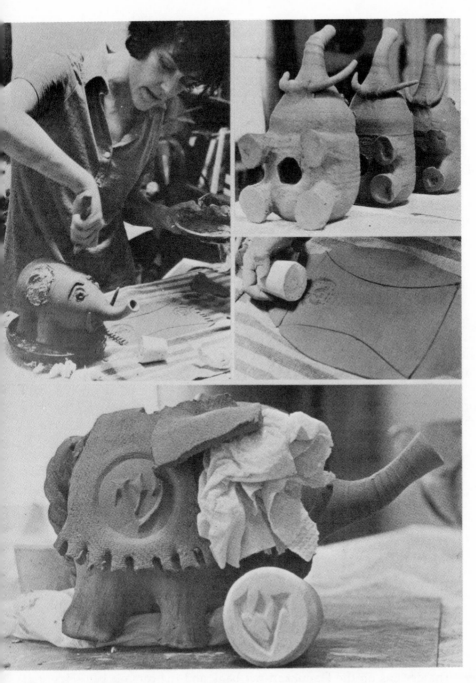

68 The elephant banks in progress.

But animal shapes are fun to work with and make nice banks; since the Maccabees triumphed over the Syrian elephant units and went on to gain independence and mint their own money, the idea of an elephant bank appealed to me. The basic form of the elephant is made from a wheel-thrown bottle shape. The neck of the bottle is bent to one side to form the elephant's trunk. If you cannot use a wheel, the entire elephant can be hand built. When the body is leather hard, the eyes and legs (1-inch-thick cylinders) are added. When the legs are firm enough to support the weight of the body without collapsing, the elephant is stood upright and the ears and the blanket added. The ears and blanket were cut from a ¼-inch-thick slab of clay which had been rolled out on a textured towel.

I used plaster stamps to emboss designs, which were derived from ancient Maccabean coins as well as Hebrew letters, into the blankets. The stamps are made by filling small paper cups with plaster of Paris. When the plaster is hard, peel away the paper and carve your design into the surface. Kitchen skewers and old dental tools make excellent carving implements. If you use letters, they must be carved into the plaster backward in order to face in the right direction on the embossed clay (see Figure 68). Plaster is so easy to carve that my daughter, then seven, carved her own name in one of the stamps used on her bank (one of the meanings of her name is "fund," so putting it on the bank was also a wordplay).

After the ears, blanket, tusks, and tail had been added to the bottle form, the coin slit was carved in the top of the bank. A round opening to retrieve the money was cut in the underside; after firing, this can be closed with a cork or a rubber sink-stopper from the hardware store.

Alexander Jannaeus
(103–76 B.C.E.)

John Hyrcanus II
(67–40 B.C.E.)

Mattathias Antigonus
(44–37 B.C.E.)

69 The designs on the Hanukkah *gelt* bank and the ceramic bell (Figure 21) are derived from the symbols on these three coins from the Hasmonean period.

70 Our cat, Tevye, a full-grown tom, looks like a kitten on top of the oversized stuffed dreidel.

Patchwork Dreidels

In recent years a new American folk art form has emerged, that of decorating and recycling blue denim workclothes. So many unusual and beautiful examples of imaginative transformations of ordinary clothing abound that the Museum of Contemporary Crafts in New York had a well-attended exhibit of them. The stuffed and appliquéed denim and mattress-ticking dreidel in Figure 70 represents a whimsical Jewish contribution to this current form of Americana.

Of the symbols most commonly associated with Hanukkah—the lamp, the *latke,* and the dreidel—the latter was the obvious choice for interpretation in three-dimensional patchwork. The finished dreidel measures about 26 inches from its point to the top of the handle and can be used as a hassock or cushion. Surprisingly, it even spins!

You can substitute your own choice of fabric, but to make the dreidel as shown you will need:

½ yard of mattress ticking
¾ yard of dark-blue denim

1 or 2 pants legs from faded blue jeans (if you have enough old blue jeans
   of different shades, you won't need to buy the dark blue denim above)
1 yard of red bandannalike material, or two 18-inch bandannas
Red crochet thread
Dacron, kapok, or other stuffing

Cut out:

2 14-inch squares of mattress ticking
2 14-inch squares of blue denim
2 equilateral triangles whose sides measure 14 inches of dark blue denim
   and two of faded denim (these will form the pyramid for the point)
4 right triangles—2 from the dark denim and 2 from the bandannas—the
   long edge of each measuring 14 inches and the 2 sides just under 10
   inches each
1 5½-inch circle of dark blue denim
A fan shape cut from a 10-by-16-inch rectangle (this was cut from faded
   denim and can be done free hand or by enlarging the pattern in Figure
   73)
The letters, cut out of the bandannas (enlarged on a grid, as described
   earlier)

Seams were sewn, then pressed flat and topstitched by hand, using heavy red crochet thread. All seam allowances are 1 inch, except for the circular top of the handle (which is ½ inch) and the letters.

Sew the 4 squares together, so each side measures 12 inches. Sew the 4 right triangles together; the long edges measure 12 inches and the sides just under 8 inches.

The letters that go on the four sides of the dreidel are: נ, ג, ה, ש; their meaning and the game are described on page 118. The same letters were used on the ceramic bell (page 62). For the lettering, enlarge the patterns in Figure 72, using the grid method. Cut the shapes from cardboard to make full-size patterns. Trace around these with a pencil on the *right* side of the bandanna fabric. Cut the letters out, leaving a ¼-inch seam allowance outside the pencil line. Turn the fabric under at the pencil line, and use any stitch you know and like to attach the letters to the sides of the dreidel in the order shown in Figure 71.

Sew together the bottom, sides, and top of the body of the dreidel according to Figure 74, leaving a seam open at the top of the cube through which to stuff it. Stuff the body, and hand-sew the open seam closed. Assemble and stuff the handle separately, and sew it securely to the center top of the dreidel.

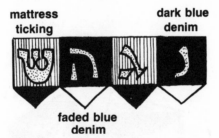

mattress ticking   **dark blue denim**

faded blue denim

71 Placing the letters on the dreidel.

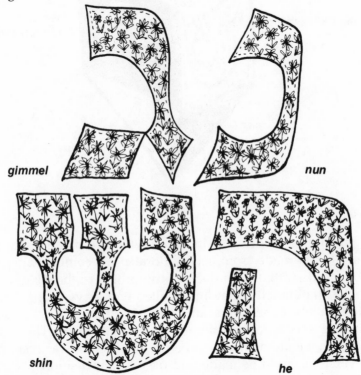

gimmel   *nun*

shin   *he*

72 Patterns for the dreidel letters.

top of handle

INSERT TO HERE
AT TOP OF DREIDEL

sewing line

73 Pattern for the handle of the dreidel.

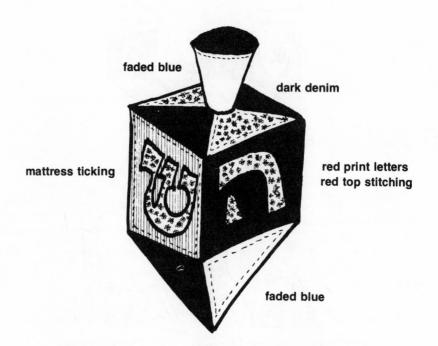

faded blue

dark denim

mattress ticking

**red print letters
red top stitching**

faded blue

74   Assembling the dreidel.

The small stuffed dreidels in Figure 70 were made using the same patterns. One is made from a blue floral print combined with a dark-blue fabric and stuffed with dacron; the other is a beanbag made from green felt with pink felt letters and is filled with navy beans. For the base of the felt beanbag the raw seams were turned to the outside and cut with pinking shears for a different decorative finish. The letters were sewn on each square by machine before the dreidel was assembled. Still smaller versions could be made and used as pincushions.

Gifts of Embroidery

Since embroidered clothes are in such demand among teenagers, an easy and enjoyable project is to embroider a design on a ready-made article of clothing, either new or old. There are any number of suitable motifs, but the shape of the article of clothing will determine how the design is laid out. I purchased a shirt and a vest and then embroidered them at home. The shirt in Figure 75 was embroidered in a herringbone stitch, following a simple pencil line drawing of interlocking *magen*

75 Embroidered shirt and vest. The needlepoint guitar strap is described in my book *The Work of Our Hands*.

Davids. The denim vest was embroidered by machine, using a close zigzag satin stitch.

The Hebrew on the vest says שלום (peace) above the double profile and אהבה (love) at the bottom. The diagram given here can be enlarged by the grid method and transferred to a piece of clothing (or cloth) by using dressmakers' tracing paper.

If you do not want to embroider an entire piece of clothing, you might consider making a patch or label that can be attached to a favorite garment. These can be of the person's Hebrew name or a single appealing motif. Worked in needlepoint, a patch label is extremely durable and can be used to identify ski clothes, luggage, or tennis rackets.

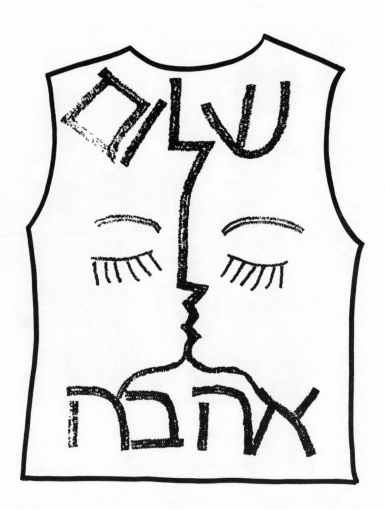

76 Vest embroidered with interlocking faces, "peace," and "love."

Necklaces

Until the Persians began to use coins throughout their empire, economic transactions were made by bartering or by using various metals computed by weight (silver being the most common) as the medium of exchange. When the Greeks arrived in ancient Israel, some of the more important hellenized city-states were granted the privilege of minting low-denomination coins; the more valuable coins were

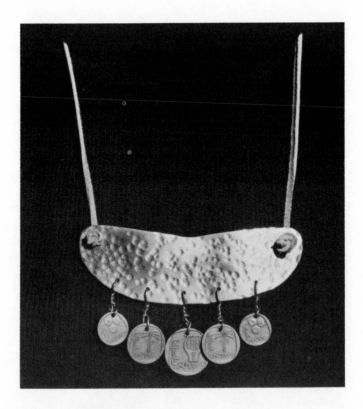

77 Necklace made from Israeli coins.

minted by the central government. After the breakup of the Greek
Empire many of the smaller states began to coin their own money.
Judea was never granted this right by either the Egyptians or the
Syrians. Those Jews of the Maccabean era who sympathized with the
hellenizers hoped that by appeasing Antiochus, they would be granted
this privilege, which would have greatly benefited their economic life.
Ironically, it was the opponents of hellenization, the Maccabees, whose
victory enabled Judea to mint its own coins, the rightful function of an
independent nation. Coins from this period have been unearthed by
archaeologists, as have Jewish coins from the time of the first war
against Rome and of the Bar-Kokhba revolt. Today modern Israel, like
any contemporary nation, mints its own coins.

When my son came back from a summer trip to Israel, he had a
pocketful of change. He made the necklace shown in Figure 77 as a
Hanukkah gift for his girl friend. The curved piece from which the coins

are suspended is brass, but it could be made from any metal, ceramic, or wood. He cut the metal and drilled the holes at his high school shop. The links connecting the parts were formed from brass wire. The pendant hangs from a leather thong.

Miniature Ritual Objects

Children learn from what they see those in the adult world doing. We are often horrified to hear some of the things they say in play, recognizing in them some of our own worst characteristics. How nice, on the other hand, when we find them playing with their toys in imitation of those things we value dearly. The miniature ceremonial objects in Figure 78 were made for my daughter's favorite doll family. The father and baby boy wear tiny crocheted yarmulkes. The *hallah* on the platter is ceramic, as are the platter and the kiddush cup. Other

78 Doll family celebrating Hanukkah.

parts of this Jewish-life-for-dolls set which are not shown include a Pesah plate the size of an ashtray with appropriate compartments, embroidered covers for matzoth and hallah, and small purchased brass candlesticks for Shabbat.

Almost any ritual object we make for our own use can be made in a child- or doll-sized version. Even smaller things (on a scale of 1 inch to 1 foot) can be created to turn an ordinary dollhouse into a miniature Jewish home, complete with tiny mezuzahs, *mizrah*, candlesticks, *hallah* cover, Pesah plate, *hanukkiah*, etcetera.

FOR THE HOME

We cannot expect our children to imitate and transmit Jewish customs and values unless we maintain these traditions in our home. Hanukkah is a joyous holiday, but it is nevertheless laced with a thread of sacrifice and martyrdom. The Maccabees did not achieve their goals without a great deal of pain. The Second Book of Maccabees embellishes the recounting of the events surrounding the first Hanukkah celebration with many tales of martyrdom. Among them is the familiar story of Hannah and her seven sons. The family was brought before Antiochus, and the children were commanded to break faith with Mosaic law and to accept the tyrant Antiochus as God or die. As their mother looked on, one after another, beginning with the oldest teenager, chose death for the Sanctification of the Name. When the eldest six had been slain, Antiochus was either moved by a shred of pity or trying desperately to win at least one tiny adherent to his cause. He turned to the three-year-old boy before him and offered to drop the royal ring to the floor; if the child would merely stoop to recover the ring, onlookers would think that he was bowing before divinity and he would be spared. But the child answered that he chose to remain united with his brothers, who had gone bravely to their death before him. His mother kissed and blessed him and she too died.

Antiochus tried to wipe out Jewish life by prohibiting the observance of its laws and customs. The penalty was death, and many paid it. While we give many gifts at Hanukkah which are totally secular and some—such as those at the beginning of this chapter—which stress the lighthearted aspect of the holiday, it is a particularly appropriate time to give presents that emphasize a commitment to the continuation of the very traditions the Maccabees fought to preserve.

Mezuzah

Many modern homes have large, almost ambiguous, passageways between rooms rather than what we think of as a standard-size doorway. Often in these places people either forget to put up a mezuzah, or they feel that the small commercially available ones look out of place and unattractive in a contemporary archway. Rather than ignore the *mitzvah*, one obvious solution is to make a mezuzah container that is both large and attractive. The one shown in Figure 79 was simply constructed by attaching a piece of stock molding (2 by 5 inches) to a larger piece of pine (3 by 7 inches) with hinges, forming a small door. Using a wood-carving chisel, a depression was gouged in the space under the door. The handwritten parchment scroll rests there, held in place by a strip of brass which is secured to the wood with a brass nail. A similar nail and a screw eye form a latch, which keeps the door closed most of the time. The mezuzah was decorated with acrylic paints in shades of yellow and white with burnt-red accents.

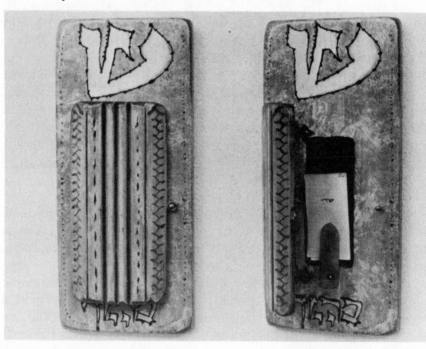

79 Painted wooden mezuzah, shown closed and open. From the collection of Rose Shulman.

Fruit Bowl

Aside from the series of benedictions which form the major part of the daily prayers, there are many short blessings (*berakhot*) that are recited to mark different occasions. Among the traditional benedictions are those said on the performance of a *mitzvah* such as lighting the Sabbath lights or putting on phylacteries; blessings of thanksgiving and praise which are said upon seeing or hearing something special (a great scholar, lightning, or the first spring bud); and the blessings before enjoying food or drink.

80 Ceramic fruit bowl. The carved letters say, "The fruit of the tree."

The blessing said before eating fruit is:

ברוך אתה יי אלהינו מלך העולם בורא פרי העץ

Blessed are You, Lord our God, King of the Universe,
who creates the fruit of the tree.

The stoneware fruit bowl shown in Figure 80 was originally made to hold applesauce for our annual *latke* party. (Although there is a separate *berakhah* for processed food, cooked apples are still considered natural enough to be included in the blessing for the fruit of the tree.) I find, however, that I use the bowl throughout the year and enjoy it especially at Rosh Hashanah and Sukkot, when eating apple slices dipped in honey is customary.

The bowl was made by draping a large ½-inch-thick slab of clay over a towel-wrapped mixing bowl. The edge of the clay was folded up and pressed against itself with a spoon handle, much as one pinches piecrust. When the clay was leather hard, I used a dental tool to carve the letters, subtly distorting the letter forms just enough to conform to the shape of the bowl but not enough to make them unreadable. The carved grooves were filled with white porcelain clay, employing the *mishima* technique used for the Hanukkah plate in Figure 36. The clay body is dark brown; the interior and part of the edge were glazed with a semigloss white glaze.

Sabbath Articles

Sabbath observance was specifically outlawed by Antiochus, as well as tyrants in other centuries, so in order to smile in the face of often bitter history, a very suitable gift for family and friends would be something with which to help them greet the Sabbath. I have made ceramic wine cups and plates, combining rough unglazed clay with the smoothness of glazed areas. One *hallah* plate had a raised pedestal carved with the Hebrew word for Sabbath, שבת. The twisted form of a wine goblet's stem suggested a grapevine.

Since Hanukkah will always have at least one Shabbat (two if the holiday begins on Shabbat), I made a special Hanukkah *hallah* cover. The batik *hallah* cover in Figure 81 was made from a 19½-by-14½-inch rectangle of cotton fabric. The corners were cut off and the remaining straight edges turned under and hemmed by machine, making the

81 White-and-blue batik *hallah* cover (finished size, including fringe; 23 by 19 inches).

cloth's dimensions 18½-by-13½-inches. Since fabric cut on the bias will not ravel, it is not necessary to turn under the diagonal edges; just continue your line of machine stitching ¼ inch in from the diagonal edge as you hem the four sides. The fringes were made of ordinary cotton string, the kind used for kites. The design of two overlapping Hanukkah lamps was lightly drawn on the fabric with a pencil and then coated with hot wax, using a brush. After waxing, the entire fringed cloth was dyed with navy blue batik dye and the wax ironed out between sheets of newspaper.

In recent years Hanukkah gift-giving has grown from the traditional few coins to include anything and everything we imagine the recipients might conceivably want. Banks that once organized Christmas Club accounts to help people begin to save for holiday expenses a year in advance now sponsor Hanukkah Clubs as well. This is perhaps an inevitable manifestation of the Americanization of Hanukkah celebration. Regardless of how much we spend or whether we buy or make the presents we give, it is important to keep in mind that the greatest gift we can give to our children (and therefore to our parents and ourselves as well) is that of transmitting our heritage.

Hanukkah commemorates both a military and a spiritual victory. When Judah and the other Maccabees rededicated the Temple, and years later when his brother Simon established the sovereignty of Judea, the victory was not merely against foreign physical enemies. It was also a triumph of the human spirit against the luring and compelling forces of materialism, uniformity, and regimentation. Since the first Hanukkah celebration twenty-one centuries ago every generation has been inspired by the eternal message of Hanukkah to resist the new temptations and tyrants which have arisen. That the people and the nation Israel survive to this day is testimony to the enduring quality of that ancient miracle. The very tenacity with which the Maccabees fought for their lives and traditions has kept us in life to this season.

"The spirit of man is the lamp of the Lord"   (Prov. 20:27)

Appendix

USING THE "ALEF-BET" FOR CRAFTS

Many of the projects in this book incorporate one or more Hebrew words in their design. The words and phrases are chosen for the additional significance they add to the object. The placement and shape of the letters are determined as much by the object's size, form, and medium as by the requirements of the particular message.

Scribes who produce pages of beautiful calligraphy must master various styles of complete and unified alphabets. This is not necessary for craft work, since you will rarely use more than a few words as embellishment. It is important, however, to be familiar with the basic structure and shapes of the letters as well as their relative sizes, because although the letter may be distorted in order to fill irregular spaces and surfaces, you would not want to inadvertently deform the letter so as to make it unrecognizable.

All European alphabets are derived from the same Semitic source as the Hebrew letters. With close scrutiny it is possible to see their common heredity. Often they appear as mirror images of the same basic form.

גG רr פP

The letters *gimel*, *resh*, and *fe*, and their "mirror images"
in the Roman alphabet

What makes them appear to differ more than they really do is the emphasis placed on the vertical line in the Roman alphabet and on the characteristic horizontal stroke, which grew out of the use of the quill, in the Hebrew.

The letters *gimel, resh,* and *fe,* showing their emphasized horizontals, with the stronger verticals of the Roman alphabet

The Hebrew alphabet is made up of twenty-two letters, all of which are consonants. Five of the letters have a different form when used at the end of the word: כ‍ך, מם, נן, פף, צץ. Five variants are created by placing a dot inside or above the letter: בב, כּכ, פּפ, שּׁש, תּת. Vowel sounds are indicated by the use of six signs made of dots and lines placed above, below, or in the center of the letter. The vowel

LETTER	NAME	SOUND	VALUE	LETTER	NAME	SOUND	VALUE
א	alef	silent	1	מ	mem	M	40
בּ	bet	B	2	ם	final		
ב	vet	V			mem		
ג	gimel	G(get)	3	נ	nun	N	50
ד	dalet	D	4	ן	final		
ה	he	H	5		nun		
ו	vav	V	6	ס	samekh	S	60
ז	zayin	Z	7	ע	ayin	silent	70
ח	het	H (often		פ	pe	P	80
		translated		פ	fe	F	
		as Ch or		ף	final fe		
		H)	8	צ	tzadi	Tz	90
ט	tet	T	9	ץ	final		
י	yod	Y	10		tzadi		
כ	kaf	K	20	ק	kof	K	100
כ	khaf	kh		ר	resh	R	200
ך	final			שׁ	shin	Sh	300
	khaf			שׂ	sin	S	
ל	lamed	L	30	ת	tav	T	400

signs are not used in the Scroll of the Law or in contemporary Hebrew newspapers and periodicals except in those intended for new immigrants to Israel learning Hebrew.

When transliterating English (or other foreign) names or words into Hebrew, you will need sounds that are not ordinarily used in Hebrew. The following system has been devised for putting foreign words into Hebrew characters. When a vowel is needed, use *alef* for A. Use *alef* and *yod* for I and E at the beginning of words. Use *yod* for Y when it sounds like the Y in "yellow" and for E and U in the middle of a word. Use *vav* for O in the middle of a word and *alef* + *vav* for O at the beginning of a word. There is no J sound (as in Jennifer) or Ch (as in Charles) in Hebrew, so the practice has grown up of using accented letters for these sounds. The J is indicated by a *gimel* that has an accent mark over it ‡ and the Ch with a similarly accented *tzadi* ‡. W, as in Wendy, is indicated with two *vavim* וו. *Tav* is used for Th, as in Theodore. Bringing ancient Hebrew into the modern world has given rise to many cross-lingual misspellings, so yours won't be the first. Remember, however, that Hebrew reads from right to left!

Syllables are traditionally not divided in Hebrew. In order to make all lines equal and have even margins on the page, six letters can be expanded horizontally. These are: *lamed, dalet, he, het, tav,* and *resh.*

Expanding letters horizontally

When planning a design using the *alef-bet*, remember to leave space for the ascending line of the *lamed* and the dropped verticals of the *kof* and the final *nun, pe, khaf,* and *tzadi*. This can be accomplished by leaving the space between the lines as wide as a letter is high. Another, more enjoyable, way—which takes more preplanning—is to juggle the lines a bit so the long verticals fit into empty spaces left in the preceding line by letters such as *yod, resh,* and *dalet*.

Spacing letters with verticals

As in all compositions, what is left out—or the negative space—is as important as the positive elements of the design. Since all the letters are not of even width, and in order to avoid either crowding or gaps, it is a good idea to keep round letters such as *pe* or *samekh* fairly close but to leave more space between letters with long verticals, such as *vav*, *he*, and *tav*. The letters need not remain in rows but can be moved around to create interesting arrangements, taking care that the letter is not destroyed by too much distortion.

When emphasizing lines, remember that Hebrews "hangs" from a horizontal bar. Either thicken the entire letter, or just the horizontals. Emphasizing the verticals is completely untrue to the nature of the characters.

Lamed and *bet*: the correct horizontal emphases appear at the left of each letter; the distorted versions, stressing the vertical strokes, at right

There is a huge difference between "Q" and "O" in the Roman alphabet; in Hebrew also what appears to be a minute difference can completely change a letter. With practice comes familiarity.

The first *alef-bet* shows the basic structure of each unadorned letter. Many variations of these skeletal forms are possible, but the basic structure must be kept in mind.

Basic structure of the *alef-bet**

Once you are certain of the particular letters in your design, cut them out of paper and move them around on the object you are making. You may find that in order to properly fill a space you have to extend a line or thicken a curve of a letter; in that case cut a new pattern piece, or tape an additional piece of paper to your original letter. With practice and patience the letters and objects will visually work together to produce a pleasing whole.

It is said that God especially loved the *alef* for its humility. It is always silent, taking its identity from those around it. So God rewarded

*Six additional Hebrew alphabets designed for crafts can be found in *The Work of Our Hands* (New York, Schocken Books, 1973).

the *alef* and gave it first place in the *alef-bet* and first place in the Decalogue. As you work with these letters, you too will develop favorites. One word or even a single letter can be worked into an intriguing design. You might decide to design a whole project around a single letter or to make a pattern by repeating it.

Modern Alef-Bet

Variations of this *alef-bet* were used for the needlepoint (Figure 30) and the fruit bowl (Figure 80).

Script Alef-Bet

The script form of the Hebrew letters lends itself very well to curved objects. It was used for the batik (Figure 22) and the *"Yom Tov"* plate (Figure 34).

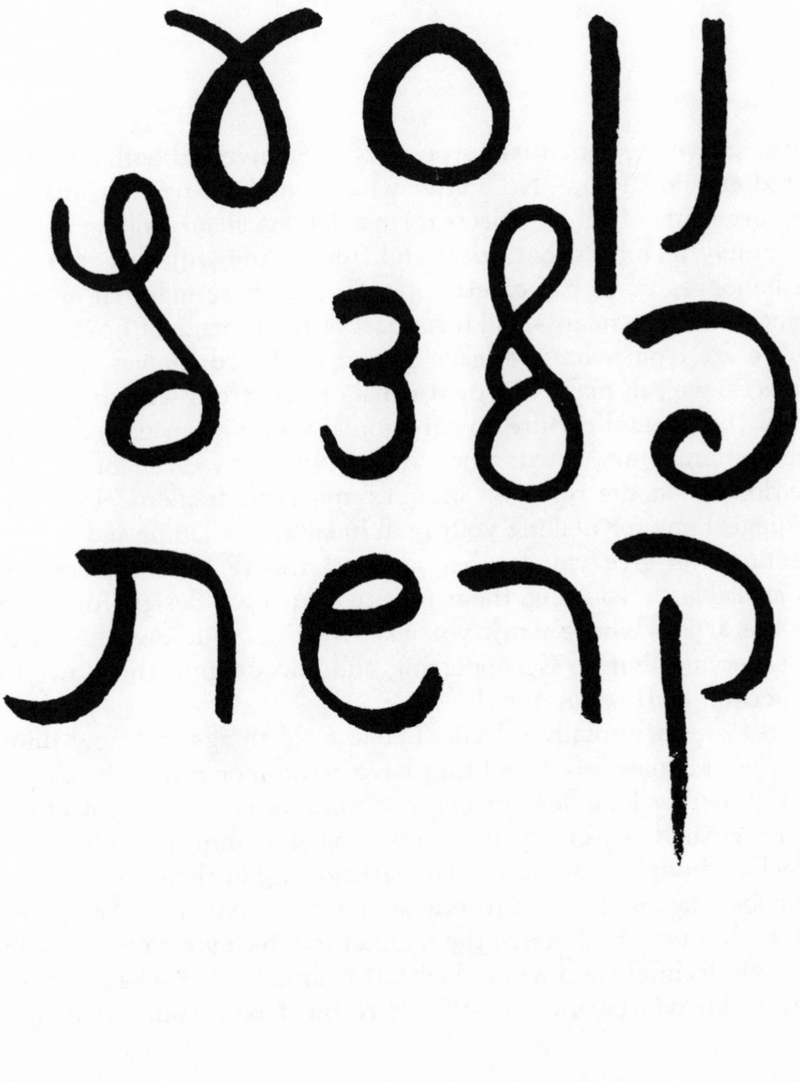

Portfolio

T he things we use for ritual purposes become invested with an almost sacred emotional aura. No matter what humble or precious material they are made of, ritual objects form a delicate chain, linking us with our family members, both past and future, and with our roots and beliefs. It behooves us to pay careful attention to these material memory carriers since our descendants will form part of their image of how we live and who we are from what we leave on our cupboard shelves. We have several choices: we can make our own ritual objects from scratch or adapt things from the general culture to ceremonial use; we can patronize and encourage contemporary artists and craftspeople; or we can buy ready-made "heirlooms" in the form of antiques and reproductions. This book contains suggestions for making your own Judaica. The lamps and dreidels in this section will give you further ideas of the variety of forms and materials available to you. Let them inspire your own designs or indeed patronize the artists whose work you like. Making your own heirlooms is deeply satisfying, but so is supporting and encouraging the flowering Jewish-American craft community!

My own tastes are totally eclectic. I collect old things and new things in many styles and materials. What they have in common is that the individual artisan—whether long dead or living around the corner—speaks to me through the created object. By using and enjoying things handmade by others I feel as though I am vicariously participating in their creation.

In his book *Megatrends* social forecaster John Naisbitt uses the formula "high tech/high touch" to describe the manner in which we have reacted to an increasingly technological world. Naisbitt maintains that whenever new technology is introduced into society, there must be a counterbalancing

82 LUDWIG WOL-
PERT: Brass, 11" high; reproduced from Museum In-
dustries New York, N.Y. for
the Israel Museum Collec-
tion (photo by Ralph Gab-
riner)

human response—that is *high touch* or the technology is rejected. The more
high tech, the more high touch is needed.

In the 1950s and 1960s high tech entered every area of our lives—our
work space (whether factory, office, store, or home), transportation, rec-
reation, health care, communication—and affected even our eating patterns
and intimate relationships. But along with automation, jet planes, television, organ transplants, CAT scans, fast-foods, and the pill we have witnessed an explosion of compensatory interest in personal development.
The human potential movement, including everything from yoga, "natural"
food, sexual and life-style experimentation to est, has mushroomed across
the country as we attempt to keep our spiritual balance in a world that
seems to be catapulting through time and space.

During this period, it seemed to me that modernization would surely
wipe out two things which are bedrock for me: "Yiddishkeit" (i.e., Jewish
cultural expression) and handcrafts. In those years *Life* magazine predicted
our demise as a people, and mass production seemed to make the individual
artisan obsolete. Then, *baruch hashem*, entered high touch. In response to
the depersonalization of machine-made objects, a craft revival blossomed all

over America. The impact of the craft movement coupled with heightened Jewish identification to produce a flowering of Jewish arts throughout the United States. A decade ago it was close to impossible to find well-designed, carefully made contemporary Judaica. True, there were a few remarkable artists such as Ludwig Wolpert, but their work was usually destined for synagogues or for the few wealthy collectors. Today the number of well-trained, talented artisans devoting their time and effort to Judaica˙ is impressive and constantly growing. While some of these craftspeople began as hobbyists primarily motivated by their commitment to Jewish life (form following functional need), increasingly we are seeing artist-craftspeople emerging from the best art and design schools in the country turning their considerable abilities to the creation of ritual objects. For some of these artists love of Judaism and art have been intertwined from the beginning; for others, their art coupled with a tentative attempt to create Judaica has led to an increased Jewish knowledge and commitment.

Just as they have in previous centuries, Hanukkah lamps and dreidels have challenged the imagination and skills of today's artists. Contemporary American Hanukkah lamps range in style and technique from ultra high-tech constructions in steel and plastics to folksy and playful ceramics. Traditional styles rendered in innovative materials are also popular. Values of antique Judaica have soared recently and frauds seem to multiply. Excellent reproductions of a variety of traditional lamps and dreidels from

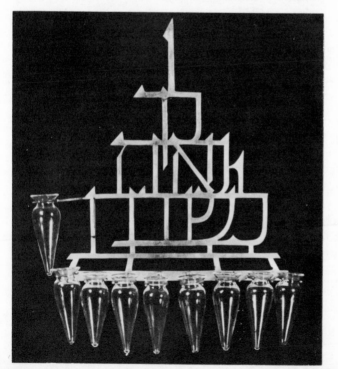

83 LUDWIG WOL-PERT: Oil lamp, nickel silver and pyrex glass on lucite holder, 8" x 8": "To praise Thee is a delight" (Courtesy Chava Wolpert Richard, The Jewish Museum, New York, N.Y.; photo by Frank Darmstaeder)

84 FRANN ADDISON: Watertown, Mass.: Brass with leaded beveled glass, 8" x 8" (photo by Robert Kaufman)

85 MOSHE ZABARI: New York, N.Y.: Embossed and fabricated silver in three parts, 11¾" wide x 6¾" high (photo by Erich Hockley)

different countries and eras are available from Museum Industries in New York City, which is reproducing objects from the Israel Museum collection.

Artists from all over the country kindly sent me their work for review for this book. I am happy to present on these pages a *sampling* of some of the most handsome lamps being made today.

Ludwig Wolpert, the Grand Old Man of Jewish ceremonial art, died a few years ago. He was a gentle, generous man who brought Jewish design from repetitious imitations of the Baroque era into the twentieth century. He left an incredible legacy, not only in the considerable body of his work, but also in the generations of artists he inspired. Artists such as Frann Addison, Bernard Bernstein, Harold Rabinowitz, Chava Wolpert Richard, and Moshe Zabari, all of whom, like Wolpert, primarily work in metal—sometimes in combination with glass or plastics—make beautiful and elegant contemporary ceremonial Judaica.

Gunther Aron, Don Drumm, Hannah Geber, Josef Fleischman, Annette Hirsh, David Klass, Stefan Siegel, Bonnie Srolovitz, and Katya Wallin are all metalsmiths. They draw their inspiration from many sources: nature, traditional motifs, Kabbalah, and from the materials themselves.

Designs in metal tend to be more formal than those in clay, which lend themselves to a certain degree of playfulness. Nevertheless, craftspeople of the caliber of Renan Burstein, Susan Felix, Edith Fishel, Nissan Graham-Mayk, Lynn Rosen, Toby Rosenberg, Claudia Schwartz, Arnold Schwarz-bart, Claire Sherman, Lynn Wachtel, and Pearl Zaltzman bring elegance

86 DON DRUMM: Akron, Ohio: "Peace Concept" in dove form *hanukkiah*, cast aluminum alloy, 15" wide x 9" high (photo by Steve Zorc)

87 JOSEF FLEISCH-MAN: c/o Elijah's Cup, Houston, Tex.: Dreidel-spice box, silver filigree (photo by Daniel Bissonet)

88 DAVID KLASS: New York, N.Y.: Tree with lions bench form lamp for oil or candles, copper and brass, 17" wide x 13" high

89 EDITH FISHEL: New York, N.Y.: "Street" lamp, porcelain

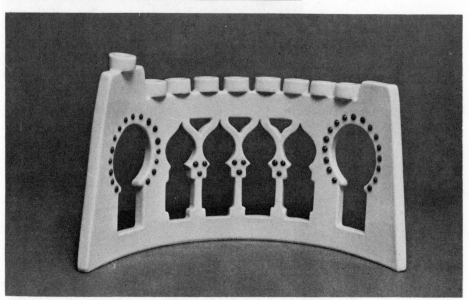

90 ARNOLD SCHWARZBART: Knoxville, Tenn.: *Hanukkiah* with moorish style "windows," architectural porcelain

and sophistication of design to this humble material. It is interesting to note that while very different from one another, Fishel, Rosenberg, Schwarzbart, and Sherman all incorporate architectural motifs into their Hanukkah lamps.

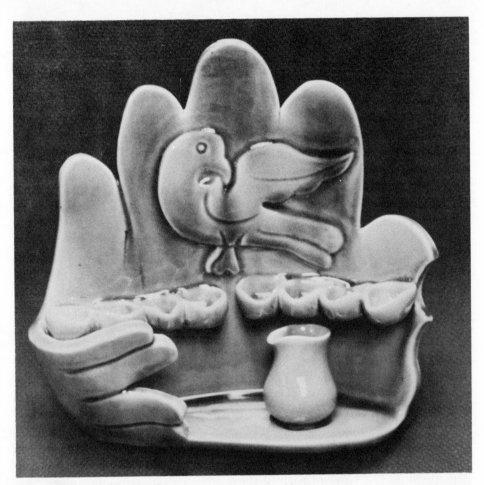

91 PEARL ZALTZMAN: Washington, D.C.: Simple yet powerful porcelain oil lamp with celadon glaze featuring dove and hamsa motifs

92 RICHARD FELD-MAN: Oakland, Calif.: Menorah form *hanukkiah*, zebrawood, rosewood, and gold plated

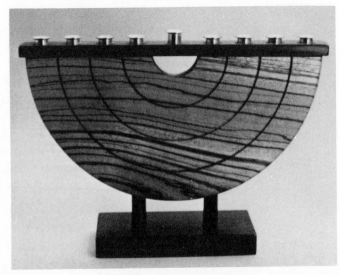

93 HERMAN BRAGINSKY: New Haven, Conn.: Dreidel, carved Vermont rock maple, 2½" x 2½" x 7"

Richard Feldman, Herman Braginsky, and Marek Kozera-Zucker work in wood, a material which adds much inherent tactile beauty to whatever is made of it. The work of each of these three artists strongly reflects their different backgrounds, as well as their considerable ability—Feldman, a California-based designer-architect; Braginsky, originally from Denmark and whose second career is art, his first having been in the heating and air-conditioning business; and Kozera-Zucker, a Holocaust survivor from Poland.

Fewer lamps are made in glass, hydrastone, or plastic than any of the aforementioned materials, but the artistry of Akrish, Harry Green, Charlotte Goldberg, and Eva Schonfield transforms these materials into very special *Hanukkiot*.

Too often we make false divisions between the "arts" and the "crafts." The diversity of technique and approach as well as the broad range of creativity and talent shown here proves beyond doubt that there are no "minor" arts and that contemporary Judaica holds its own alongside the finest secular art being produced in America today.

Index

179